The All-Weather
RETIREMENT
PORTFOLIO

The All-Weather
RETIREMENT
PORTFOLIO

Your Post-Retirement
Investment Guide to
A WORRY-FREE INCOME FOR LIFE

The
WORRY-FREE
RETIREMENT
Series

Randy L. Thurman
CFP®, CPA/PFS

ForbesBooks

Published by ForbesBooks, Charleston, South Carolina.
Member of Advantage Media Group.

ForbesBooks is a registered trademark, and the ForbesBooks colophon is a trademark of Forbes Media, LLC.

Printed in the United States of America.

10 9 8 7 6 5 4 3 2 1

ISBN: 978-1-95086-353-2
LCCN: 2021920519

This custom publication is intended to provide accurate information and the opinions of the author in regard to the subject matter covered. It is sold with the understanding that the publisher, Advantage|ForbesBooks, is not engaged in rendering legal, financial, or professional services of any kind. If legal advice or other expert assistance is required, the reader is advised to seek the services of a competent professional.

 Advantage Media Group is proud to be a part of the Tree Neutral® program. Tree Neutral offsets the number of trees consumed in the production and printing of this book by taking proactive steps such as planting trees in direct proportion to the number of trees used to print books. To learn more about Tree Neutral, please visit **www.treeneutral.com**.

Since 1917, Forbes has remained steadfast in its mission to serve as the defining voice of entrepreneurial capitalism. ForbesBooks, launched in 2016 through a partnership with Advantage Media Group, furthers that aim by helping business and thought leaders bring their stories, passion, and knowledge to the forefront in custom books. Opinions expressed by ForbesBooks authors are their own. To be considered for publication, please visit **www.forbesbooks.com**.

To my lifetime clients, past, present, and future ...
you are the reason I do this work.

To be sure, there are more important things
in life than financial security.

But if I can help you breathe more easily because
of my help in this area, then I have succeeded.

Also by
Randy L. Thurman:

*The Worry-Free Retirement Guide to
Finding a Trustworthy Financial Advisor*

*More than a Millionaire: Your Path to Wealth, Happiness,
and a Purposeful Life—Starting Now!*

One More Step: The 638 Best Quotes for the Runner

Get Rich Slowly ... but Surely!

Do You Have Questions about the All-Weather Retirement Portfolio?

Visit Retirement Investment Advisors, Inc., at TheRetirementPath.com to access these free resources:

A retirement calculator

Want to know how much it takes to retire? How long will your savings last? Are you on the right track to reach your goals? We have several calculators ready for you to use, free of charge. Check them out here: TheRetirementPath.com/Retirement-Calculators.

White papers and other useful info

Discover our white paper comparing our Thrift Savings Plan to the All-Weather Retirement Portfolio. This is a more detailed version of Chapter 9. Explore so much more: https://rebrand.ly/TSP.

A subscription to our newsletters

Our weekly and monthly newsletters are packed with market news, helpful financial information, and insight into our advisors. Keep in touch here: https://rebrand.ly/RIAsubscribe.

Your free initial consultation

Thinking about retiring or wondering when you can? Schedule your complimentary consultation with a CFP® professional. No strings attached. Submit your request at TheRetirementPath.com/Contact.

Information about our firm

Our team is always ready to assist you with your retirement decisions. Learn more about our background and expertise: https://rebrand.ly/ RIAteam.

Still Have Questions for the Author?

Contact Randy L. Thurman through his firm's website at TheRetirementPath.com.

Contents

PART III.

Designing Your All-Weather Retirement Portfolio

PART IV.

Ready to Set Sail

Introduction

I was visiting with my dad. He was a former high-school football coach. With his hard-nosed approach, he made his players say, "Yes, sir," and, "No, sir." He made them make good grades, show respect for their teachers, and be accountable. He loved coaching. Although he never made a lot of money, he loved being a positive influence in young men's lives. Truly, the man was a success.

It had been a rugged year. Dad's health was failing him, and he needed 24-hour, 7-day-a-week care. I made the difficult decision to put him in a high-level, skilled-care retirement facility. It's so tough seeing your dad, a man's man, slowly go downhill. As we chatted across the small table in the corner of his room, our conversation turned to his favorite topic—me. He asked me why I still worked. The question was one of curiosity but also concern. Life is short, and I, as he liked to tell me, was not getting any younger. He knew I didn't have to work for financial reasons. So why?

My response was, "Why did Michael Jordan keep playing basketball? He didn't have to." I explained that I still worked for three reasons. I love what I do. I feel that my work matters. And I make a great income that allows me to give a good chunk to charity—and sometimes that makes all the difference for those organizations. It also lets me do some extra nice things for my family, which makes all of us happy.

I could tell Dad was proud of my response. The moment has become a treasured memory.

My dad has since passed away. But as J. M. Barrie said, "God gave us memory so that we might have roses in December." This memory of my dad, and countless other moments like this, are part of his legacy to me. It's something that survives beyond his lifetime.

It's my hope that this book will be my legacy, to help you and others like you, far beyond my time here on earth. While I'm still around, though, and continue to work, I hope it will bridge the time and distance between us. As I share my 35 years of experience and knowledge—and constant learning—my goal is to help you worry less about money so you can enjoy your retirement more. Much more. This, in turn, will help you gather your roses, your memories, your legacy for your loved ones.

It is the heart and soul of my work.

What's New in the Second Edition

This new edition of *The All-Weather Retirement Portfolio* stands on the shoulders of the first. It builds on what came before, and allows us to see beyond our original horizon. Life experience tells us that rough weather will inevitably come our way, but with the right preparation and the smartest tools we can ride out every storm. Here's how this second edition will help you sail on to sunnier days.

1. I analyzed a much larger sample size, with data that now goes back to 1930.

For the first edition of *The All-Weather Retirement Portfolio* there was excellent data available going back to 1970, which allowed me to analyze how all segments of the financial market performed starting at that point. We had limited data starting from when the markets were created in 1926, but not for all asset classes. In that first edition I used the available information to assess the performance of each segment of the portfolio.

Since then, a lot more information has become available. A financial services company called Global Financial Data has compiled data on the performance of every major asset class offered in the financial markets, going all the way back to 1930. Needless to say, that's an enormous amount of information not previously available, and I made full use of it in this second edition. I was able to analyze data for a full 90 years for every asset class I considered, including in the portfolio offered here.

For example, when I wrote the first edition of this book, it was impossible to find data on the performance of stocks in international and emerging markets prior to 1970. Today, thanks to the new resources offered by Global Financial Data (and a large check from me), that information is now available. With the new data I was able to do a complete analysis of various portfolio configurations starting in 1930. That increased my sample size substantially. And of course, a larger sample size means more reliable results.

2. I focused like a laser on what's most important: How long will your money last in the worst financial storms?

The goal of the All-Weather Retirement Portfolio is to provide you with income for 40 years. That's based on the assumption you'd like to retire at age 60 and live until you're 100.

As I'm sure you can imagine, there are endless ways to assess market data, and unlimited factors to consider. Risk and return probably come to mind, and without a doubt those are critical. But when all is said and done, and once all the numbers are crunched and all the spreadsheets have been scrutinized, all that really matters to you is this: You want your money to last as long as you do.

That's why I kept my analyses focused—first, last, and everything in between—on that one criterion. All the assessments I ran to create this edition were designed to evaluate the portfolio against that singular goal—the portfolio had to be able to ride out every financial storm and provide an income for 40 years. As you'll see in the pages that follow, this new All-Weather Retirement Portfolio does exactly that.

3. I examined every 40-year time frame since 1930.

When I created the first edition of this book, I had complete data going back to 1970, but very limited data for market performance prior to that period. For that reason, I looked at a single 40-year time frame, starting in 1973, and built a portfolio that would last the full 40 years. Why 1973? Because that was the worst year the market had seen since 1970. The portfolio passed with flying colors, demonstrating that the portfolio—as it appeared in the first edition of this book—was strong enough to provide an income *for that particular 40-year period.*

With the additional resources from Global Financial Data, covering every asset key class since 1930, I was able to look at every 40-year time frame in the past 90 years—and there are 51 of them. That means, once again, we have a much larger sample, by a factor of 51, to assess the strength of the portfolio. With that information, we now have an even better All-Weather Retirement Portfolio that would have continued to provide income for 40 years, even if you'd retired *in any of the worst years the market has seen since 1930.* That includes the years 1937 and 1969, the worst years the market has seen in the past 90 years.

More data, more time frames to evaluate, more financial storms. The end result? A stronger plan than before.

4. I've created an improved portfolio with even greater diversification, so it weathers the financial storms better than ever.

With the trove of data that's become available in recent years, I was able to test the historical performance of smaller segments of the market, where information was sorely lacking before. For example, I analyzed segments of the bond market that aren't commonly included in standard portfolio recommendations. I've been recommending them to my clients for some time based on my 35 years of experience and evaluation. I knew those assets had some rocky years early on, particularly around the time of World War II, but I've seen them perform well in more contemporary times. Even so, without hard data to back up my evaluation, I refrained from including them in a book like this—until now.

Now that the hard data is available, and I've done the number crunching to confirm my own assessments, I can share those recommendations with you. You'll see some of them included in the basic All-Weather Retirement Portfolio—in fact, we start building the portfolio with intermediate corporate bonds, which were not included in the first edition of this book. There are other new additions, including some I offer as enhancements to the basic portfolio in Chapter Thirteen. I'm pleased to be able to make all that information available to you now.

5. I've added a new lifeline to help you sail safely through the worst financial storms.

With the more diversified asset allocation in this new edition, I've built a portfolio that would have lasted 40 years in all but the worst 40-year time frames in our 90-year test period. But this is your retirement income we're talking about. There are no do-overs, and there is little margin for error. That's why I added one more element of protection—let's call it a lifeboat you can use in the event of a truly catastrophic financial storm.

To make sure the All-Weather Retirement Portfolio passes the test in *every* time frame the market has ever seen, it now includes an added safety measure you can apply if the perfect financial storm occurs early on in your retirement, when your portfolio is most vulnerable. I call it the "8-Year Rule." It's a simple, easy-to-follow strategy you can apply during the first 8 years of your retirement if—*and only if*—your account balance takes a serious hit as a result of a turbulent market during that critical time. If it does, you can apply the 8-Year Rule and enjoy your worry-free retirement with confidence your portfolio will continue to generate income for as long as you need it.

Although the quest for the perfect All-Weather Retirement Portfolio is unending, based on all the information available to us now—and, to be sure, there's a great deal of data available—this portfolio performs above and beyond anything else I've seen. It's the culmination of my 35-plus years of experience, plus new (and expensive) data, enough spreadsheets to fill a checked luggage bag (plus a carry-on), and countless hours of research, all distilled down to create the information I offer you in this book.

It's my hope that you'll accept this offering, and my belief that it will carry you safely through any storm you may encounter in the years to come, so you can enjoy a rewarding, restful, inspiring, and truly worry-free retirement.

—Randy L. Thurman, 2021

PART I.

Preparing to Set Sail into All Kinds of Weather

Chapter One

The Perfect Financial Storm

Are You and Your Retirement Portfolio Prepared?

For more than 35 years I've been helping people invest so they can enjoy smooth financial sailing throughout their retirement years, through all kinds of financial storms. It can be done. But like any successful journey it requires a good map, smart navigation, and a sensible route.

You see, many investment plans can deliver great retirement income *if* the economy is booming. But the income strategy you'll discover in this book has delivered consistently, *regardless* of what the economy has done. How do I know this? Because I've looked at every single rolling 40-year time frame since 1930, and I can tell you the plan you are about to see passed the test of time for investors like you, who need a worry-free income for life.

Why are those time frames so important? Because that's how long you need your money to last. Whether you want your portfolio to generate income for 40 years or not, you need to know that this plan has weathered every storm the market has seen in the past 90 years, to provide a solid, consistent income stream.

Not only do I want you to have a plan that stands the test of time, I also want you to have as much income as possible, so you can embrace life and enjoy your retirement years to the fullest. I want you to do the things that matter to you, while you're still able to do them, without running out of money in your later years. It's a tricky balance. Finding the *right* balance means you'll have peace of mind as you enjoy your retirement now and for the rest of your life ... without worrying about money.

> Finding the *right* balance means you'll have peace of mind as you enjoy your retirement now and for the rest of your life... without worrying about money.

Just like a well-planned journey, the right investment plan is based on an understanding of how to allocate your resources among the various options available to you. You won't need a cruise ship to take your grandson paddling around the lake on a Sunday afternoon, nor would you want to cross the ocean in a canoe. Knowing how much energy—or cash—to allocate to each type of vehicle will help you survive the perfect storm, whether you're 1,500 miles out at sea or 15 years into your happy retirement. I'll show you exactly how to build your portfolio using the right investment vehicles in the right amounts for smooth sailing—and a worry-free income for as long as you need it.

Finally, any good plan includes a strategy for dealing with challenges if and when they arise. The thing is, the financial market is not all sunshine and gentle waves all the time. There are times when stormy weather rolls in and the market suffers a major setback. The All-Weather Retirement Portfolio is strong enough on its own to enable you to ride those out … nearly every time. But if a severe downturn happens during the first 8 years of your retirement—right after you stop putting money into your retirement accounts and start taking money out—it could spell real trouble, because that's when your sustained income is most vulnerable. If that downturn becomes what I call a "perfect financial storm"—an event so severe it's happened only three times in the past 90 years—you'll need to know how to handle it. Don't worry, I've got you covered. I'll show you what to look for, and when to drop anchor if one of those rare storms hits. More importantly, I'll show you when to raise that anchor and continue on, as if nothing had happened.

Of course, none of this is an absolute guarantee of future financial security—such a thing does not exist. But I think you'll agree the research I've done makes a powerful case for the strength of the All-Weather Retirement Portfolio. That's the value of testing it against every financial storm the market has seen since 1930.

Perhaps the following story will show you what I mean.

When Linda[1] came into my office she was a picture of health. She was 62 years old, and had worked 20 years for a company that had been bought out by a larger corporation. New management had come in and wanted to make the company "more efficient." This meant downsizing, consolidating jobs, and working employees harder and longer with less pay. Linda found she didn't enjoy getting up and going to work anymore. She was ready to retire.

She wanted to know her options. Like most people in her position, she wanted as much income as possible to spend and to live comfortably. On the other hand, she didn't want to run out of cash.

---

1   "Linda" is a composite of several investors. She makes it possible for us to explore a variety of real-life scenarios in one conversation.

She had done some research, and learned a bit about certificates of deposit, stocks, bonds, mutual funds, annuities, and Treasury bills. She'd read magazines, newsletters, and books, and listened to gurus, brokers, and advisors on TV and podcasts. They all had advice and it all looked pretty good. And everyone had something different to say.

Most of the advice was all about getting the best return. But a voice inside her head said, "If it sounds too good to be true ..." And what about risk?

At the other end of the scale was advice that was geared completely toward safety. That seemed sensible, but she knew she couldn't live on the meager amount of income those recommendations would provide, and they didn't seem to protect her against inflation.

What to do? Linda was an intelligent woman with a lifetime's experience in a lot of different areas, but investing wasn't one of them. She understood there were many variables to consider, but she knew she didn't have the knowledge to evaluate them all. Stocks, bonds, mutual funds, certificates of deposit ... the effect of world events on the economy, interest rates, and the stock market—it all seemed pretty overwhelming, and made her feel uncomfortable.

She shifted her weight in the chair across from mine, thought for a moment, sighed, then looked me straight in the eye. "Now that I'm finally ready to retire, I want to be able to enjoy myself. The last thing I need is to have to worry about all this investment business, and I certainly don't want to worry about money every time I think about going out to dinner," she said. "I want to travel, spend time with my grandkids, volunteer with the youth groups at the Y ... there are so many things I've been looking forward to." She stopped. She was thinking about her dream retirement. "Heck, I'll probably be busier when I stop working than I am now. I'd sleep a lot easier if I felt confident I'd have a nice, steady income for the rest of my life—

enough to be able to spend money on the things I've been looking forward to for the past 20 years."

She leaned in. "Can you help me with that?"

"Yes, Linda, I can," I answered.

I explained to her that there are two approaches to investing: investing to accumulate wealth and investing for dependable income. Choosing the right approach is all about matching her investment strategy to her needs at this time in her life.

The first approach is the one that usually comes to mind when people think about investing: They think about a plan aimed at building a large nest egg with enough money to become financially independent. They think of big killings in the stock market. This kind of investing can yield high returns, but it also involves great financial risk. If you're young, have many earning years ahead of you, and can afford a big potential loss, maybe that's appropriate. But as Mark Twain said, "There are two times in a man's life when he should *not* speculate: when he *can't* afford it and when he *can*."

Since Linda was coming to the end of her employment years, she couldn't afford to risk her life savings. She needed to look at the second kind of investing: investing for income. In other words, she needed to invest her money in a way that would give her the best possible opportunity to have a worry-free income for the rest of her life.

I understood her needs and her concerns. Over the years, I've heard them thousands of times, and I've spent much of my career researching the best strategies to address them. I explained to Linda that, based on decades of experience working with retirees just like her, I knew I could help her with an investment strategy that was right for her.

She seemed to relax a bit. "That sounds like what I've been looking for, Randy," she said. "I don't need any fancy bells and whistles at this stage of my life. I just need a steady, reliable income. So what's next? Where do I put my money so it will work for me?"

I explained, "You begin by focusing on the investment vehicles that give you the right balance between risk and return, then you use them in the right way. Just like a good travel plan, a good worry-free income strategy starts with the right vehicle. I use mutual funds."

"I've read about them. But honestly, it's not clear to me exactly what they are," she said.

"That's okay, I can help you with that. What's most important for now is that you understand what you're doing and why," I responded. "Mutual funds are a way for you and many other people to pool your money into a single fund, and let a professional invest it for you in a variety of different stocks or bonds or both. When you're part of a larger pool of money like that, you have buying power on par with the big boys. At the same time, you avoid the risk that comes with putting all your eggs, or dollars, in one basket, as you would if you were using all your money to buy a single stock or bond.

"For example, when you invest in a company's stock, you own a piece of that company—it's a tiny piece, but it does mean you actually are one of many, many owners. If the company's stock goes up, you do well. Invest in the right one, at the right time, and you can make a killing. Then again, if the company you own stock in goes under, you lose that money you invested.

"If a company you own stock in goes belly-up, it doesn't affect you nearly as much if you own it inside a mutual fund. That's because you may have five hundred or more other stocks inside the fund to make up for the loss, or at least to water it down. With mutual funds you lose the chance for the big killing, but you gain staying power.

"When it comes to investing at this point in your life, Linda, it all starts with choosing the right vehicles, like mutual funds," I explained.

"That sounds simple enough," she said.

I chuckled. "Great! But it does get a bit more complicated. There are thousands of mutual funds out there, with different types of assets and different levels of risk and reward. The real key to success is knowing which *types* of funds to choose, and in what proportions. It's a little like a food recipe. If the recipe calls for a half teaspoon of salt, and instead you put in two tablespoons of baking powder, the result will taste awful. If you're just learning to cook, you can start from scratch and test various formulas, make some mistakes, learn from them, and finally come up with a great recipe. Or you can examine what others have done and follow their recipes. Even better if you use recipes from the most famous, most successful chefs in the world. Their time-tested recipes work again and again, and you get to enjoy the results."

Linda laughed. "Oh, Randy, if you only knew—I love to cook and I love to play in the kitchen. Just don't ask me to stick to a recipe—that's no fun at all! Sometimes I get great results. But believe me, I've had my share of disasters!"

I smiled and nodded. "Well, the successes certainly sound like lots of fun, and I'm sure you'll be playing in the kitchen a lot more when you have more time to enjoy it. But I know you're not interested in playing and improvising when it comes to your money. An investment recipe tested against decades of data will save you time, money, and potentially a great deal of heartache.

"Let's take it one step further. If you do cook with a recipe, the one you choose depends on whether you want breakfast or dinner, right? Well, it's the same with investing—choosing the right strategy depends on whether you want to accumulate wealth or provide yourself with a reliable income.

"Have you had enough, or would you like me to keep going?" I asked.

"Please keep going. But first, there's something I don't understand. Why is investing for income so much different from investing for wealth? If I get a good return, won't that take care of all my problems?" Linda asked.

"Great question," I answered. "I've touched on investing for wealth, when your return on investment is your primary concern. But the vehicles that provide the best return often carry the greatest risk. When you focus on return alone, you could be in danger of losing the money you invested in the first place. I like to quote Will Rogers on this one. He said, 'I'm not as concerned about the return *on* my investment as I am the return *of* my investment.' Investing for income takes both into account—risk as well as return. That's why it's different from investing for wealth. It's a plan that allows you to enjoy your retirement without worrying about your money."

Linda sat back and smiled broadly—she realized this was a plan that made sense for her needs at this pivotal moment in her life.

And for this pivotal moment in *your* life, I've prepared this guidebook to help you plan your own course. In the coming chapters we'll take a closer look at why the strategies for investing for income are the ones that make sense for you as you enter your retirement years. We'll also look at the nuts and bolts of investment vehicles, so you'll have a better understanding of what you're buying and why. Most important, you'll find a simple, market-tested strategy for investing successfully to generate an income that will sustain you for the rest of your life—even if the market goes south and you need to ride out a "perfect storm" in the national or global economic climate.

But first things first. Let's begin by taking a look at where you are today. What preparations have you made? What strategies have you already put in place? Are they the best ones for you? Where do you need to make some changes to set you on the best possible course?

Turn the page, and we'll start exploring the answers.

Chapter Two

Are You Ready to Retire?

A Quick Checklist

L ike Linda, you're about to enter a new phase in your life, one that could last up to 30, 35, 40 years—or more. That may be as much time as you've spent working! If you've begun to prepare for the big event, you know there's a long list of decisions and choices to be made. Moreover, the decisions you make at this point in your life could affect how well you live throughout the leisure years ahead. With solid information and a sound strategy, you can make the choices that will ensure your investments provide the life and lifestyle you've been looking forward to.

> With solid information and a sound strategy, you can make the choices that will ensure your investments provide the life and lifestyle you've been looking forward to.

Just How Well Prepared Are You?

Before we go any further, let's take a look at what you've done to prepare for your retirement, and find the areas where you need more information so you can make the right choices from here on. Take a moment to complete the Retirement Readiness Test. It's a good place to start, so you'll have a better sense of what your particular needs are as you read through the chapters that follow.

Just answer the questions on the next few pages, then total up your points to calculate your readiness rating.

Retirement Readiness Test

1. Do you know how much you can expect to receive in Social Security benefits?

   ▫ Yes (10 points)

   ▫ No (0 points)

2. Have you decided when to take Social Security benefits? That is, will you take them immediately or defer them? If you plan to defer, have you decided when you'll begin taking benefits?

   ▫ Yes (10 points)

   ▫ No (0 points)

3. Have you decided where you want to live?

   ▫ Yes (8 points)

   ▫ Have it narrowed down to two or three places (3 points)

   ▫ No (0 points)

4. Have you prepared a spending plan for your retirement years, including health-related expenses?

   - □ Yes (8 points)

   - □ No (0 points)

   - □ Kind of (2 points)

5. When did you last review your life and health insurance?

   - □ 3 months ago (12 points)

   - □ Within the last year or 2 (6 points)

   - □ More than 2 years ago (0 points)

6. When did you last update or review your will?

   - □ Within 6 months (12 points)

   - □ Within 2 years (8 points)

   - □ More than 2 years ago, but less than 5 years (4 points)

   - □ More than 5 years ago (2 points)

   - □ What will? (-5 points)

7. If you're married, is your spouse retired or planning to retire?

   - □ Already retired (8 points)

   - □ Planning to retire (4 points)

   - □ Haven't decided (0 points)

   - □ I'm single (8 points)

8. Have you determined how you will provide for long-term healthcare needs for you and your family?

   □ Yes (12 points)

   □ Somewhat (6 points)

   □ No, I haven't considered it (0 points)

9. Have you figured out how much income you will need for a comfortable retirement?

   □ Yes (12 points)

   □ Somewhat (6 points)

   □ No, not really (0 points)

   □ No, I'm just depending on Social Security (-4 points)

10. Have you determined what your net worth is? If so, how recently?

   □ Yes, within the past 12 months (12 points)

   □ Within 2 years (8 points)

   □ Within 3 years (5 points)

   □ No, or more than 3 years ago (0 points)

   □ I don't own a net (-25 points)

11. How diversified are the assets you're counting on to generate your retirement income? (Check all that apply.)

   □ Certificates of deposit (CDs) or money market—amount equivalent to 3 to 6 months of your monthly expenses (3 points)

   □ Individual stocks: Large companies (5 points)

   □ Individual bonds: Government or high-quality bonds (5 points)

   □ Mutual funds: Small company, value stock funds (5 points)

   □ Mutual funds: Large company, value stock funds (5 points)

   □ Mutual funds: Large company, growth stock funds (5 points)

   □ Mutual funds: Bond funds (5 points)

   □ Mutual funds: International stock funds (5 points)

12. Have you decided what you'll do with the money in your company pension plan?

   □ Yes, I'll roll it over into an IRA (8 points)

   □ Yes, I plan to take monthly payments (6 points)

   □ Yes, I'll take the distribution in cash (2 points)

   □ No (0 points)

   □ I don't have one (0 points)

13. Which professional advisors have you consulted to help you make the transition to retirement? (Check all that apply: 5 points each)

   □ Attorney

   □ Certified Financial Planner™

   □ Registered investment advisor

   □ Insurance representative

   □ Tax planner or preparer

   □ Real estate agent

14. Have you thought carefully about which hobbies, interests, or work you will pursue in retirement?

   □ Yes (10 points)

   □ No (-5 points)

15. Are you actively gathering information about health, lifestyle, living arrangements, and financial aspects of retirement?

   □ Yes (10 points)

   □ No (0 points)

How Did You Do?

0 to 60 points. You're like most people on the verge of retirement: You haven't thought much about it. Nothing is wrong with that, but you do need to start planning immediately. Read this book cover to cover and get going!

60 to 110. You've made a little headway, but should start getting serious about planning. Start reading this book now. You can skip any sections that address issues you've already covered thoroughly.

110 to 160 points. You've got a pretty good handle on retirement. But, to be sure you're on your way to a worry-free income for the rest of your life, you will need to develop a long-term strategy for asset allocation that will ease the impact of taxes and inflation on your portfolio. Pay special attention to Chapter Nine, "Ten Steps to a Worry-Free Income for Life," a solid strategy for building a retirement income portfolio. How does it match up with yours? Are there any changes you need to make? Also review Chapter Twelve, "Finding an Advisor You Can Trust," to be sure you have the best possible crew on board to help you monitor your portfolio and ensure it's always balanced to meet your needs. The right professionals can also refer you to other specialists in their networks to handle any other issues that need attention.

More than 160 points. You're on the right track, and doing a lot of things the right way. Congratulations! But just to be sure, go over any chapters that cover matters you don't feel certain you addressed. And of course, it's always important to have a solid team of professionals to back you up when you have questions or need additional advice about investments or other matters. Take a close look at Chapter Twelve, "Finding an Advisor You Can Trust," to help you find the support you need or make sure your present team meets the most important criteria, and will be there to help you navigate through any surprises that may come your way. Then get ready for a retirement plan that can weather the storms and keep you on course for a worry-free retirement!

Chapter Three

Charting Your Course

Seven Questions You Need to Ask

Linda and I were just beginning to discuss the nuts and bolts of investing for retirement when she started to fidget in her chair. She looked worried.

"There are so many things to think about," she said, "and it's all so new to me—I just don't know where to start."

"Well," I replied, "we'll start at the beginning." I pulled out my notepad and made a list—the seven questions you must ask as you prepare to build a comfortable income for life:

1. How much are you starting with?

2. How long do you want your money to last?

3. How much do you want to end up with?

4. How much return will you get on your investments?

5. How much risk should you take on?

6. Will my income keep up with inflation?

7. How much do you want to take out each year?

I showed Linda the list, and together we went over each item one by one.

How much are you starting with?

After a lifetime of spending and saving and investing, how big is your retirement nest egg? In essence, this is everything you have that is going to generate retirement income for you. Tally up your CDs, annuities, investment accounts, IRAs, pension, and other retirement plans—all the accounts and funds that will be used for your retirement income.

How long do you want your money to last?

What is your life expectancy? According to actuarial tables, a single person aged 60, living today in the United States, has a life expectancy of 25.2 years.[2] A couple, both age 60, has a *joint* life expectancy (an estimate for the one who'll survive the longest) of 30.9 years.[3] That number can vary depending on exactly where you live, family medical history, your own health, your ethnicity, and a long list of other factors. But even if you research the most precise actuarial data, your life expectancy is just an average—you've got a 50:50 chance you'll live longer than that. So if you plan to have your money last only until you reach your life expectancy, you've got an even chance of outliving your income. What kind of plan would that be? A better strategy aims to have your money last at least 40 years, so you'll have an income to support you through your 100th birthday.

---

2   "2020 Single Life Expectancy Table," Ed Slott and Company LLC, https://www.irahelp.com/printable/2020-single-life-expectancy-table.

3   "2020 Joint Life Expectancy Table," Ed Slott and Company LLC, https://www.irahelp.com/printable/2020-joint-life-expectancy-table.

How much do you want to end up with?

Would you like to have some money to leave your kids, your church, your alma mater, maybe even the local animal shelter? Or do you just want to enjoy every dollar you've worked so hard for, like the old pro Saul Bloom in *Ocean's Eleven* who says, "I want my last check to bounce." Either way, the real issue is that it's better to have money left over than to run out. After all, the best thing you can do financially for your kids is make sure they don't have to support you. So plan to end up with enough of a cushion so that, if you live longer than you expect, you'll still have enough money to be comfortable.

How much return will you get on your investments?

It's impossible to predict exactly how much you can earn across the decades of your retirement years. But in the coming chapters we'll look at how you can blend different types of investments to create what I call an "efficient" portfolio—one that maximizes your expected return while taking on the least degree of expected risk. As you'll see, the strategy is quite a bit different from the one you've used to accumulate your nest egg. But it's one that will put you in a position to feel confident your money will continue to work for you while you're out enjoying those golden years.

How much risk should you take on?

Once you begin taking money out of your retirement fund, it becomes far more sensitive to the volatility of the market. A sudden downturn in the value of your investments can have a much bigger impact on you now than it would have while you were putting money in—especially if that downturn happens in the first 8 years after you retire. We'll look at some examples, so you'll understand exactly why this is so. But you can relax. Remember, I've done extensive research to uncover the ways to protect you from the perfect financial storm, so you can weather a squall akin to anything we've seen in the modern-day financial market—that includes the horrendous downturn of 2008 as well as 1937, 1969, and 1973, the worst years to start drawing retirement income—and anything you're likely to see throughout the 40 or so years of your retirement.

Will my income keep up with inflation?

One thing you can be certain of is that the value of your money is likely to change over the next 40 years—your dollars will probably buy less as time goes on. It's a hidden factor that can blindside you if you don't include it in your plan. But of course, I'll show you how to protect yourself from that, too.

How much do you want to take out each year?

As much as possible, of course. But finding the number that will ensure your money lasts as long as you do, even if you encounter the perfect financial storm along the way, takes all of these seven key questions into account. We'll take a closer look at how you arrive at that number in Chapter Six, "Income for Life: Make the Most of Your Retirement." For now, let's just say you can make an informed decision about how much you'll take out in your first year of retirement—and adjust it annually to accommodate a rising cost of living—so that you can enjoy your money and retirement without sacrificing your peace of mind.

These seven simple questions cover the key issues you need to consider as you plot your course for smooth sailing throughout your retirement. In the coming chapters we'll go over all the information you'll need to answer these questions, and put together the strategy that will provide a worry-free income in virtually any economic climate.

PART II.

The Longitude and Latitude of Investing after You Retire

Chapter Four

Investments 101

With our seven key questions in front of us, we were beginning to get a handle on the decisions Linda needed to make and the information she'd need to make the *right* decisions. She seemed to be breathing a little easier.

"Okay, that makes sense," she said. "But before I can decide how much money to take out, I need to make sure my money is invested in the right places, don't I? You said that risk is a bigger concern for me now than it was when I was putting money *into* my retirement account."

"That's true. And you'll decrease your risk by creating a portfolio with the right investments in the right combination."

"How do I know which investments are risky and which ones aren't?" Linda shifted again in her chair. "I mean, it just seems that when it comes to investing … well, I just don't think I have enough experience to make smart choices."

I replied, "I think it was Will Rogers who said, 'Heck, we're all smart or ignorant, just in different areas.' You'll feel a lot better when you understand the basics, and some simple principles that will help you decide where to put your money and how to take it out. That way you'll have a better handle on what it takes to generate an income that will take care of you for the rest of your life."

"Sounds good to me." She nodded.

"Okay. Let's start with an overview of the different types of investment vehicles, then we'll look at each category and talk about what's good and bad about each one." I proceeded to lay out a foundation of information that would give Linda—or an investor like yourself—the knowledge and confidence to develop a solid strategy.

Basically there are three broad categories of investments:

- Guaranteed cash investments

- Fixed long-term investments

- Equity investments

Guaranteed cash investments are the simplest, and most everyone has them. They are just what the name suggests. You are guaranteed that at some point you will be able to take out the amount of money you put in. In a sense, you can count on your "cash" always being there for you. You earn a small amount of interest, but the fair market value of your investment doesn't change. If you need the money quickly, you can get to it with little or no penalty. Examples of guaranteed cash investments include:

- Checking accounts

- Savings accounts

- Money market accounts

- Certificates of deposit, or CDs (those that are short term, a year or less)

- Treasury bills (These are similar to bonds, but because you hold them for a very short term—12 months or less—and therefore their value fluctuates very little, they function more like cash in your portfolio.)

The second type of investment, a **fixed investment**, is nothing more than a loan you make in return for a fixed amount of interest. The loan can be to an individual or an institution, but the quality of the investment depends on the credit rating of the borrower. There are many different entities you can loan to; some have good credit ratings, and some not so hot. Examples of fixed investments include:

- **Corporate bonds**. With a corporate bond, you loan money to a corporation—not to be confused with a stock, with which you own a piece of a corporation. (See below for more detail on stocks and other "ownership" investments.) Bonds are safer than stocks because, in the event the corporation runs into financial trouble, bondholders get paid before stockholders.

- **Government bonds**.

- **Certificates of deposit, or CDs**, those that are long term, greater than a year.

- **Preferred stock**. Preferred stock is a safer investment than regular, or "common" stock, because if a company falls on hard times it will pay dividends on preferred stocks before common stocks. However, unlike common stocks, preferred stocks behave like a fixed investment because the dividend is fixed in advance and never changes, much like a bond.

The third type of investment is the **equity investment**. Equity means ownership. Your home, or any other real estate you own, would be an equity investment. Stocks would be another. When you own a stock, let's say AT&T, for example, you own part of that company.

How much you own depends on the number of shares you have and the amount everyone else has.

So far, so good—it's pretty simple, and there are lots of options to choose from. But with investments, there are always trade-offs. Let's look at these three types and talk about what's good and what's bad about each of them.

Guaranteed Cash Investments

A guaranteed cash investment guarantees that your principal will always be there for you, and that you'll receive a specified amount of interest, so it gives you a "feel-good" factor. You know you'll never have less than you invested, and because of the guaranteed interest rate you feel as if you are always making money. Also, the investment is liquid, which means you can get to your money quickly, without loss of principal.

But remember, there's always a trade-off, and in this case it has to do with something we call the "real rate of return." That's the value of the interest you've earned *after* you 1) pay taxes on it and 2) adjust for increases in the cost of living. With guaranteed cash investments the interest rate is usually so low that, after taxes and inflation, your real rate of return is often negative. So while your principal will always be there for you, the *value* of your investment actually decreases.

For instance, if you earn 3% interest on a CD[4] and you pay taxes at 33%, then out of your 3% earnings, 1% will go to Uncle Sam (33% of 3% = 1%). So after taxes your net earnings are only 2%. The annual increase in cost of living for retirees like you (it's more for retirees than for working folk, mostly because of increased healthcare costs)

---

4   I know you're probably not earning 3% on CDs these days, but it's a nice round number that makes it easy to illustrate my point.

is currently about 4%. When you subtract that from your after-tax interest earnings of 2%, then you are effectively losing 2% on your investment every year.

That may not seem like a big deal at first. But in effect, you've signed up for a guaranteed loss rather than a guaranteed income. And when you compound a guaranteed loss over your life expectancy, you end up living on about a third of what you started with. That's one reason why I believe the biggest risk you have on your investments and income stream is the increase in the cost of living. So yes, the potential loss you can incur with guaranteed cash investments is a big deal.

Even so, you need to have money you can get your hands on when you need it, and savings accounts, CDs, Treasury bills, and the like are good vehicles for that. Generally, you want 3 to 6 months of your monthly expenses—commonly called a cash reserve—to be in guaranteed cash investments.

Fixed Investments

As we've said, a fixed investment is basically a loan, usually to a bank, a corporation, or the government. Bonds are among the most common types of fixed investments. The entity issuing the bond agrees to pay a fixed amount of interest for a stated time frame. It then gives you back your principal at the end of the loan period, which is when the bond "matures." If you *don't hold* the bond to maturity, it has a value that could be more or less than what you paid for it. (More about this in a minute.)

The value of your fixed investment, or loan, depends on many things, including:

- how interest rates have fluctuated since the loan was issued,

- the creditworthiness of the entity,

- the length of the loan.

Generally speaking, the better the creditworthiness of the entity, *the lower the interest*—you take less risk, but earn less money because of it. Also, in most times, the longer the loan, the higher the interest rate. There are some exceptions.

One of the reasons it's important to include bonds among your investments is that their value goes up when the value of most other investments is going down. Unfortunately, that also means their value might go down when other investments are doing well. How can that be?

Let's look at an example. Say you purchased a bond worth $10,000 that pays 10% interest. A year later interest rates go up and there are nearly identical bonds paying 11%. If you try to sell your bond, will anyone want to buy yours at 10% when they can get 11%? Not anyone who's thinking clearly. Then what do you have to do to motivate people to buy yours? Since you can't change your interest rate, you have to lower your price to, say, $9,090. If interest rates continue to go up, then the value of your bond continues to go down. The longer-term bonds have more risk associated with them, because they have a longer time frame to pay out interest at a certain rate, so there's a greater likelihood interest rates in general will go up during that time. So if rates go up, long-term bonds take the biggest hit in value.

On the other hand, if you have a bond earning 10% interest, and rates in general go down, let's say to 8%, you'd be able to ask a higher price because people will be looking for a chance to earn that 10% rate. You might get as much as $12,500 for a bond that originally cost you $10,000. But you also benefit from holding on to that bond, because the dollar amount of interest never changes—if you were getting a $500 interest check every 6 months, you will continue to get it.

This fluctuation in value, based on changes in interest rates, is what we call "interest rate risk." Interest rate risk is the reason why bonds aren't as liquid as cash investments. You can generally convert to cash fast, but you may take a loss in principal.

Default is another risk associated with bonds. Remember, your bond is in effect a loan you made to the company that issued it. If the company runs into trouble and is on the verge of bankruptcy, it may default on that loan and fail to pay back your initial investment or your interest—which means you stand to lose *all* your money.

So why would you want to buy a bond when you can buy a CD or money market account, which guarantees you'll never lose your principal? The good thing about bonds is that they almost always pay a higher interest rate than guaranteed cash investments. Because of this, they don't carry as much risk that you'll lose purchasing power, due to that "real rate of return" issue we discussed on page 40. Remember, that potential loss of purchasing power is virtually guaranteed with cash investments. The risks associated with bonds may or may not come to pass.

You can minimize your risk of default by choosing entities with solid credit ratings. I wish I could tell you how to avoid the risk associated with rising interest rates. Sorry to say, predicting interest rates is much like predicting the stock market in the short run—it's virtually impossible to do.

Now, in addition to bonds, there are other types of fixed investments. And there are different entities that you can loan money to. For example, bank certificates of deposit, or CDs, are basically loans to the bank that are FDIC insured up to a certain amount. You can get them in different maturities. I consider CDs that have maturities longer than a year to be fixed investments. (Remember, we covered shorter-term CDs under "guaranteed cash investments" earlier.) Because your principal is protected by the FDIC (up to a certain amount), these are generally safer than bonds, but the interest rates are lower.

Equity Investments

While bonds and long-term CDs might be called "loanership" investments, equity is an "ownership" type of investment. You put your money into a vehicle of your choice, and in return, you own something—with all the perks and problems that can entail.

If you're like most people, when you think of "equity" you think of real estate—your home, or maybe rental property you own. Historically these are good investments, however there's one problem: they're not liquid. If you need money, you can't count on being able to sell a piece of real property quickly. There are investments called "real estate investment trusts" (REITs) that try to eliminate the liquidity problem by pooling your money with that of others to buy shares in real estate investments. However, REITs are relatively new on the market, and there's not a lot of data available that tracks how they move relative to the real estate market in general. Because of this, I don't recommend them as part of your retirement portfolio at this time.

What I do recommend is the other type of equity investment we all know as common stocks, essentially a share in a corporation. These are a little more complex than CDs or real estate, but they play an important role in your overall strategy.

When you buy a share of common stock, you also gain equity in that you own part of the company. It's a small part, true, but you still own it. As an owner you have certain rights: voting rights in proportion to your percentage of ownership, the right to receive your percentage of the dividends, and so forth. You also stand to reap financial benefits because the value of your shares, over time, tends to go up. In fact, odds are the value will go up more than inflation, so stocks usually provide a good hedge against that inevitable drain on your portfolio.

When you own stock, the return on your investment comes when the company pays you dividends (usually paid quarterly), and when the price of the stock increases so that you can sell your shares for more than you paid for them. The combination of dividends plus the increase in the price of your shares is called "total return."

The downside is that stocks tend to be more volatile than other investments; if the value of the stocks goes down, so does the value of your investment. It means that if you wanted to sell your stock, you might not be able to get as much as you paid for it. This can happen for two reasons. First, there's what we call "business risk"—if the company you own stock in performs poorly (for example, if product sales drop dramatically) your stock performs poorly as well. The profit margin might disappear or the company might even lose money, or the business can fail completely and the value of your stocks could fall to zero. The other reason your stocks might go down is called "market risk"—the price of shares goes down even though the business is doing well. It might be due to an unanticipated fall in that market sector (remember the dot-com bust we saw in 2000?), a hot news story that sends investors running the other way, or any number of nebulous factors that are impossible to predict. Whatever the reason, the volatility of the market is particularly important if you are investing for short periods of time, generally five years or less. That volatility is usually less of a problem over longer periods of time.

The amount of volatility you're likely to experience with a given stock varies too, depending on the type of company issuing the stock. For example, small companies (also called "small cap," which is short for "small market capitalization") tend to be more volatile than large companies ("large cap"), but in the long term they usually give you a higher return. You also have "value" oriented companies and "growth" oriented companies. Growth companies pay little or no dividends because they plow their profits back into the company. But the expectation is that their earnings—and as a result, their value—will grow more than the average company, and that will be reflected in what you can sell your ownership, or shares, for. Value oriented companies tend to pay you a higher dividend every quarter. However, these companies are often "out of favor" with the investing public. This can be caused by a variety of factors, but most often it's because they have not been providing a strong return on investment. They also tend to be more volatile than the growth companies.

So, the four types of stocks can be sorted into the following grid:

	LARGE COMPANY	SMALL COMPANY
VALUE	Large Cap, Value	Small Cap, Value
GROWTH	Large Cap, Growth	Small Cap, Growth

Each of these types of stocks moves differently—that is, they increase or decrease in value—in different economic climates. By creating a portfolio that includes a careful balance of stocks from the various groups, you can maximize the probability that your investments will provide you with a sustainable income for the rest of your life—regardless of what happens in the economy at large. I'll show you exactly how to create that balanced portfolio in Chapter Nine, "Ten Steps to a Worry-Free Income for Life."

When I had this discussion with Linda, she made the same assumption most retirees do, one that causes them to make a serious error in their investment strategy. She said, "But I'm retiring. I don't really have time to plan for a return on my investments, do I? I mean, there's no point in investing in stocks that are good for the 'long term' at this stage of my life, is there?"

"Yes, there is," I told her. "For one thing, you may be retiring today, but you're not going to spend all your money this year—or next. So your time frame for investing is actually quite significant. In fact, it's longer than your life expectancy."

"Seriously? Why would it be longer?"

"Because life expectancy

> By creating a portfolio that includes a careful balance of stocks from the various groups, you can maximize the probability that your investments will provide you with a sustainable income for the rest of your life—regardless of what happens in the economy at large.

is just an average. You're 62 now, and your life expectancy is 85 years, or 23 years from now—but remember, that's just an average. That means you've got a 50% chance you'll live longer than that. So even though you're retiring, your money still has to work for you for a long time. Sure, you'll be taking a portion of your money out as income every year. But the rest of it will continue to generate funds to provide income for many years to come."

Linda nodded in agreement.

What's important for you to know is that you *do* need to invest for the long term, and while the volatility of equity investments makes them risky in the short term, they're an important part of your strategy for your long-term retirement income.

Still, I realize that by now it may seem like you're stuck between a rock and a hard place. If you're like most of us, you like the higher returns of stocks and bonds, but can't stand the thought of losing your money. Is there a way to get the earning power of fixed and equity investments, and eliminate the default risk of bonds and the business risk of stocks?

Not completely. But you can *virtually* eliminate business and default risks through a thing called mutual funds.

Mutual Funds

Mutual funds are a method of investing in many different stocks or bonds all at the same time. Essentially, you pool your money with a lot of other people, then give it all to a professional investment manager who invests this large pool of money for you. Mutual funds come in different flavors, depending on the types of investments they hold. Usually a fund specializes in one of the three investment types: cash, fixed, or equity.

When you invest in a mutual fund, you virtually eliminate default and business risks because you spread your money out across many different entities. For example, a single mutual fund might have thousands of bonds in the fund. That way, if a few of the bonds default, you couldn't care less because it impacts you very little. You have effectively diversified away the default risk. A stock mutual fund works the same way in diversifying away business risk.

What about the interest rate risk associated with bonds? You can reduce that somewhat, but because all bonds tend to be affected in the same way when interest rates fluctuate, the associated risk will be there to a certain extent no matter what you do. Still, in a fund that's diversified among a large number of entities, and among long-term and short-term bonds, your money is safer than when you invest in any single bond.

The same is true of the market risk associated with stocks. Because the market tends to move in one direction or the other, particularly within certain categories of stocks, it's impossible to eliminate the risk associated with a downward shift in the price of your shares. Still, the diversification of a mutual fund can shield you from an abrupt downturn in any one corporation or market sector.

The downside here is that with mutual funds—whether they're cash, fixed, or equity funds—you will never hit a home run. These vehicles don't offer the chance you'll pick the next Apple Inc. and make a killing. Because you have so many stocks in a fund, no single stock can make the entire fund hit big numbers. But remember, a huge loss on a single stock won't break you, either.

You must decide what is most important to you. You can try to hit the home run, and if you miss, you get wiped out. Or you can protect yourself against business risk and default risk, and live with a more modest return on your investment. Since you're already at retirement age, chances are protecting your income stream and purchasing power are the big priorities. If so, then mutual funds are the way to go.

There's one more layer of protection available to you through mutual funds. By investing in several different types of mutual funds you can minimize the impact of market risk on your retirement income. Remember, the bond market tends to go up when many other investments are going down, so if your equity fund is struggling, your bond fund may help keep you afloat. If you also diversify among funds investing in different types of equity stocks, like the ones we discussed on pages 45 and 46, so much the better.

Putting It All Together

In just a few pages we've made a good case for the benefits of including both fixed and equity investments in your strategy for your retirement income. But a clear understanding of *what types* of equities and fixed investments you need, and the formula for building a crash-proof income for life, is where we're headed. For now, though, you've made a good start just by knowing the basics, because the more you know, the more you can feel confident in the plan we'll put together in the pages that follow.

The most important part of investing for an income that can withstand a crash is knowing how to blend, or diversify, your investments among the different types. You diversify among a selection of stocks and bonds, then diversify further among different types of stocks and different types of bonds.

"My dad used to tell me not to put all my eggs in one basket." Linda chuckled as we wrapped up our first meeting.

I agree. In the coming chapters we'll talk about the different types of baskets, and how many eggs to put in each one.

Chapter Five

Investing for Income Is Different

In the years leading up to retirement, your primary goal is to build as large a nest egg as possible. Now that you're ready to retire, your investment goals shift from *building wealth* to *generating income from the wealth you already have*. This presents challenges you may not have considered before—but it's critical that you do. The techniques that are most effective for accumulating your nest egg can result in a bag-lady future if you continue to apply them after you've had your retirement party.

Investing to Accumulate Wealth: Dollar Cost Averaging

When you were investing to accumulate wealth, your number one concern was return on your investment. Of course, you kept an eye on the level of risk, but because time was on your side you could afford to consider riskier, more volatile investments, like the stock market—and get the benefit of the higher returns often associated with those investments. One of the techniques that make that possible is a thing called "dollar cost averaging" (DCA)—investing the same number of dollars at regular intervals. In fact, with dollar cost averaging, a volatile market and the risks associated with it can actually work in your favor. DCA also makes sense before retirement because, chances are, you're allocating some portion of your income to your retirement fund each year.

But once you retire, you no longer have the benefit or protection of dollar cost averaging, because you may not be generating new income to invest each year. In fact, you'll be taking money out of your investment fund—now *that* will become your income. In this scenario, all the parameters change. Suddenly the volatility of the stock market has the potential to devastate your retirement fund, and dollar cost averaging won't save you. A more stable portfolio is the better choice, even though it doesn't offer the chance to hit a high return. You'll still put your money in a combination of fixed investments and stocks, but we'll use a formula that's designed specifically for your needs at this time in your life. Let's look at some specifics.

Imagine two different portfolios: Portfolio A is highly volatile, while Portfolio B is more stable. For the sake of argument, assume they both average a 10% return over 5 years.[5]

---

5   In case you're the analytical type, this is arithmetic average, not geometric.

YEAR	PORTFOLIO A	PORTFOLIO B
1	-30.00%	10.00%
2	-30.00%	10.00%
3	10.00%	10.00%
4	50.00%	10.00%
5	50.00%	10.00%
5-Year Average:	10.00%	10.00%

Even though the 5-year average return is the same for both of these portfolios, your net results vary dramatically depending on whether you're in pre-retirement mode, making regular deposits, or at retirement, investing your nest egg all at once. Let me show you why.

Suppose your niece is in her pre-retirement years, and she decides to invest $20,000 a year for five years—that's dollar cost averaging. She's careful with her money, and considers putting it in a vehicle that pays a guaranteed return year after year, like Portfolio B.

But her financial advisor steers her in a different direction. After their meeting, your niece chooses, wisely enough, to invest in the stock market, Portfolio A. She realizes she'll assume some risk in the market's inevitable ups and downs, but she also expects a pretty good return over time. Remember, she's dollar cost averaging, so when the market goes down, she invests the same dollar amount as when the market is up. This allows her to buy shares at a lower cost, so she purchases *more of them* than when they're priced higher. Then, because she's in it for the long haul—she has several years before retirement—when the market does turn up, she'll have a larger number of shares increasing in value. The net result of dollar cost averaging is that *the more volatile the market, generally the better she'll do over time.*

Take a look at how your niece's investments did in Portfolio A:

PORTFOLIO A: MORE VOLATILE INVESTMENTS

Year	Annual Investment	Account Balance at Beginning of Year	Earnings	Account Balance at End of Year
1	$20,000	$20,000	-$6,000	$14,000
2	$20,000	$34,000	-$10,200	$23,800
3	$20,000	$43,800	$4,380	$48,180
4	$20,000	$68,180	$34,090	$102,270
5	$20,000	$122,270	$61,135	$183,405

Not bad. Now let's see what would have happened if she'd "played it safe" with Portfolio B:

PORTFOLIO B: LESS VOLATILE INVESTMENTS

Year	Annual Investment	Account Balance at Beginning of Year	Earnings	Account Balance at End of Year
1	$20,000	$20,000	$2,000	$22,000
2	$20,000	$42,000	$4,200	$46,200
3	$20,000	$66,200	$6,620	$72,820
4	$20,000	$92,820	$9,282	$102,102
5	$20,000	$122,102	$12,210	$134,312

In her case, even though both portfolios averaged the same return over the 5-year period, in the volatile market your niece made an almost 40% greater return on her investment. She actually added nearly $50,000 more to her retirement fund than she would have with a steady rate of return. That's the power of dollar cost averaging.

Investing for Income: Reverse Dollar Cost Averaging

But your situation is different. Suppose you've just popped the cork on that champagne bottle, said goodbye to your co-workers, and headed for the golf course. You've officially moved beyond the days of dollar cost averaging. You're no longer building your retirement fund—you're ready to begin spending it. You have a $100,000 nest egg (let's keep the numbers simple) to invest in one lump sum. Should you put it in that volatile portfolio that did so well for your niece? Or would you be better off choosing something with a steady rate of return? Here's what happens to a lump sum investment in your niece's Portfolio A:

PORTFOLIO A: MORE VOLATILE INVESTMENTS			
Year	Beginning of Year	Earnings	End of Year
1	$100,000	-$30,000	$70,000
2	$70,000	-$21,000	$49,000
3	$49,000	$4,900	$53,900
4	$53,900	$26,950	$80,850
5	$80,850	$40,425	$121,275

And here's what happens if you choose Portfolio B:

	PORTFOLIO B: LESS VOLATILE INVESTMENT		
Year	Beginning of Year	Earnings	End of Year
1	$100,000	$10,000	$110,000
2	$110,000	$11,000	$121,000
3	$121,000	$12,100	$133,100
4	$133,100	$13,310	$146,410
5	$146,410	$14,641	$161,051

In your case, the more stable investment vehicle nets you about a 30% greater return than the volatile market, or an additional $40,000, give or take. Because dollar cost averaging is no longer part of your strategy (and you're not buying lots of shares when market price is down), those negative returns in the early years of Portfolio A really hurt. Clearly the strategy that works best for you, now that you're investing for income, is different from that of your niece, while she's investing to accumulate wealth. While volatility worked for her, it's a landmine for you.

And the impact becomes even greater when you begin drawing money out of your account. In effect, you apply a principle we call "reverse dollar cost averaging"—taking money out at regular intervals rather than adding to the pot—and the results can be devastating. Let me show you what happens to your portfolio when you do. In the following examples we'll start with an initial distribution rate of 5.5% (I'll explain why we use that rate in Chapter Six, "Income for Life: Make the Most of Your Retirement," beginning on page 229) taken at the beginning of each year. Then, to maintain your spending power at that level, we'll increase your distribution each year by an amount equivalent to the inflation rate—we use 3% here, since that was the average rate of inflation between 1930 and 2019.[6]

With Portfolio A, the bottom falls out pretty quickly when you start taking that distribution:

PORTFOLIO A: MORE VOLATILE INVESTMENTS				
Year	Beginning of Year	Distribution	Earnings	End of Year
1	$100,000	$5,500	-$28,350	$66,150
2	$66,150	$5,665	-$18,146	$42,340
3	$42,340	$5,835	$3,650	$40,155
4	$40,155	$6,010	$17,073	$51,218
5	$51,218	$6,190	$22,514	$67,541

But it's quite a different scenario with Portfolio B:

PORTFOLIO B: LESS VOLATILE INVESTMENTS				
Year	Beginning of Year	Distribution	Earnings	End of Year
1	$100,000	$5,500	$9,450	$103,950
2	$103,950	$5,665	$9,829	$108,114
3	$108,114	$5,835	$10,228	$112,506
4	$112,506	$6,010	$10,650	$117,146
5	$117,146	$6,190	$11,096	$122,051

That's right. With the more stable investment portfolio you'd find yourself with *more than 80% more money* at the end of 5 years than if

---

6   The actual average annual inflation rate from 1930 through 2019 was 3.1%. For our purposes here I've rounded it to 3.0%.

you'd chosen the volatile market in our example. That's why volatility, or risk, is such a critical factor when you're investing for income. Once you make the switch from dollar cost averaging—putting money in each year—to reverse dollar cost averaging—taking money out—you sail into a radically different financial climate.

The All-Weather Retirement Portfolio is designed to handle that risk, to make sure you'll have a worry-free income for life even when you switch from dollar cost averaging to reverse dollar cost averaging— when you stop putting money into your retirement account and start taking money out. The strategies I'll show you are so powerful they've survived the perfect financial storm in 96% of rolling 40-year time frames since 1930. As for the remaining 4%—just two events since 1930—I have a plan for those, too. I call it "the 8-Year Rule," and I'll tell you all about it and when to use it in Chapter Nine on page 125.

But what about that distribution amount? How do you know how much money you can take out, so you can enjoy your retirement years and still feel confident you'll have a worry-free income for life?

Here's some good news for you: It may be more than you've been led to believe. Turn the page and I'll tell you why.

Chapter Six

Income for Life

Make the Most of Your Retirement

I t's probably one of the most important decisions you'll make when you retire: How much will you withdraw annually from your retirement assets? Take out too much every year and you may have to seriously reduce your standard of living later in life, to avoid depleting your assets. Take out too little and you may unnecessarily reduce your standard of living from the start, so you're not able to enjoy your retirement as much as you'd like.

Where's the balance?

There are a variety of factors to consider when we calculate your withdrawal rate. They include:

- your life expectancy,

- your expected long-term rate of return on your investments,

- the anticipated inflation rate, and

- how much principal you want to have left at the end of your life.

The easiest piece of the puzzle is deciding how much you want to leave your heirs. Okay, it's not easy, but it's up to you—you can choose the number you'd like to build into your plan. For our purposes here, we'll assume you want to leave nothing—spend it all while you can. If you wish to leave the kids something, you can plug that number in when you make your own calculations (probably with your financial advisor).

Unfortunately, life expectancies, rates of return, and inflation are difficult to predict over a retirement period that can span decades. Here are a few guidelines.

Your Life Expectancy (It's Longer Than You Think!)

How long does your money need to last? How many years will you need to support yourself? While it's easy enough to find out your actuarial life expectancy, those numbers are only averages. Here's how much longer the National Center for Health Statistics (NCHS) thinks you're likely to live:

LIFE EXPECTANCY [7]		
Your Age Today	Males	Females
50	29.9	33.5
55	25.7	29.0
60	21.8	24.8
65	18.1	20.7
70	14.6	16.8

---

7   Elizabeth Arias and Jiaquan Xu, "United States Life Tables, 2018," *National Vital Statistics Reports*, 69, no. 12, November 17, 2020, https://www.cdc.gov/nchs/data/nvsr/nvsr69/nvsr69-12-508.pdf.

However, as we discussed in Chapter Three, approximately half the population will live longer than tables like this suggest. Knowing how long your close relatives lived and how healthy you are can help you gauge your life expectancy. But just to be safe, it's a good idea to plan to live … some would say, to 100. That's especially true if you'll need income to support two people, such as you and your spouse. The NCHS calculates a "joint life expectancy" for such situations. For a couple, both at age 60, the joint life expectancy is 31.8 years. You can see why it's so important to build an extra cushion into your plan for how long your money will need to last.

Expected Rate of Return

Making a realistic assessment of what your investments will do for you over the next 30 to 40 years or so is a little like trying to skip a stone across the surface of a pond. It's easy to shoot too high or too low, and if you don't get it right you get more of a *kerplunk* than a nice rhythmic hop. One way to get a feel for how much your portfolio can earn is to look at how investments like yours have performed throughout the modern financial era—that means you need to consider the data since 1930. These historical rates of return aren't perfect reflections, but averages taken over defined periods of time. But we don't just take those averages at face value—we want to be more conservative than that, and assume you'll earn a rate of return that's lower than long-term averages. Of course, even if you get the average return correct, the *pattern* of actual returns—that is, one that includes the ups and the downs in your earnings month by month—can have a significant impact on your portfolio's balance, just as it did in Portfolios A and B in our discussion in Chapter Five. But remember, this is about providing you with a worry-free income, so we'll factor that potential impact into our strategy by looking at returns from *the worst times the market has delivered for retirees* since 1930—just in case you encounter a similar pattern after you retire.

Expected Inflation

This is the hidden factor that can eat away at your spending power as the years go by. Since 1926, inflation has been as high as 18.16% in a single year—that was in 1946. We've seen it at staggering rates as recently as between 1973 and 1982 when it averaged 8.67%. Rates have been relatively tame recently, averaging just 2.10% per year between 2000 and 2020.[8] Still, I feel we're in for a bout of higher, troublesome inflation in the near future. Even at tame levels, inflation can have a dramatic impact on your money's purchasing power over time. To make sure you don't feel that impact during your retirement years, we'll want you to increase the amount of money you withdraw each year by an amount equivalent to the rate of inflation.

Your Optimum Worry-Free Retirement Income

So, what is a reasonable percentage to withdraw on an annual basis? Opinions vary, but let's start by looking at some of the research out there. One study concluded that to ensure your assets last for 30 years your initial withdrawal rate should be no higher than 3%, with

---

8   Roger G. Ibbotson, "The Long-Run Perspective," *2021 SBBI Yearbook: Stocks, Bonds, Bills, and Inflation: US Capital Markets Performance by Asset Class 1926-2020,* Appendix C-7.

subsequent withdrawals adjusted for inflation.[9] But 3% means your cash flow will be less than it needs to be, which means you won't enjoy that money while you have the chance. And is 30 years long enough? As we saw in Chapter Five, you could reasonably expect to live longer than that. What happens in year 31?

Let's take an approach that offers a significant improvement in your retirement income, so your income lasts longer than 30 years even though you take a larger distribution—while still protecting your portfolio. By mixing different types of investments together, investments that have dissimilar movements in different economic climates, and including some basic income rules from year to year, I'll show you how you can expect your income to last 40 years *with an initial withdrawal rate of 5.5%*, adjusted each year to keep pace with inflation.

And I'll take it one step further. I'll show you how the retirement investment and income plan I've developed would have performed across every 40-year time frame since 1930. You'll see that with the 5.5% initial distribution rate, adjusted each year for inflation, *the plan is successful 96% of the time*. My "8-Year Rule," which I'll show you in Chapter Nine (page 125), will take care of the remaining 4%. I think you'll agree this is an income strategy that truly has the potential to change your quality of life throughout your retirement.

The plan you'll learn here will give you the peace of mind of knowing you've done all you can do, even if you don't have a crystal ball. It gives you the maximum probability that no matter what happens in the outside world—even if the perfect financial storm

---

9   Philip L. Cooley, Carl M. Hubbard, and Daniel T. Walz, "Retirement Savings: Choosing a Withdrawal Rate That Is Sustainable," *AAII Journal* 10, no. 3 (February 1998): 16–21, www.aaii.com/journal/article/retirement-savings-choosing-a-withdrawal-rate-that-is-sustainable?utm_source=sitesearch&utm_medium=click, accessed August 15, 2014.

comes your way—you'll know you have done everything possible to have a worry-free income for life. That's our goal—and a worthy one at that.

Chapter Seven

The Perfect Financial Storm

Can You Survive It?

W hen times are good, there are all sorts of investments and investment styles that provide a nice income stream. When interest rates are high and the stock market is booming, it's easy to look like a financial wizard. In that environment we rest easy at night knowing our money is working hard for us.

But what if the stock market crashes? What if interest rates plummet, so your CDs earn a paltry 0.5%—or even less? Will your nest egg be able to provide you with the income you need to survive, let alone the comfortable retirement you've been working toward for all these years? Is it all a big gamble? Or is there a way to protect yourself in the face of whatever financial storms you're likely to encounter in the future?

Take a deep breath, and put your worries aside. We're about to run things through the financial gauntlet—that "perfect financial storm" we've been talking about—and test a variety of investment vehicles to see how they would have performed if you'd retired just as the storm clouds were gathering. (Remember, your retirement income is most vulnerable in the early years of your retirement. That's because you don't have time to recover from a loss, and because of the impact of reverse dollar cost averaging. If you need a refresher, refer back to Chapter Five, "Investing for Income Is Different," starting on page 51.) 1973 was one of the worst years the market has seen since 1930, when we started recording extensive data on market performance, so we'll use that as our starting point. We'll see what happened to each type of investment during the 40-year period from 1973 through 2012.

I'll tell you right now, the results aren't pretty. But they'll lay some groundwork to help you see why the strategies I'll show you later in the book are so important—and so effective. While the investments we'll look at in the pages that follow fall short in providing income for as long as you're likely to need it, take comfort in knowing *there is an approach that can survive anything the market has dished out since 1930.* Before we're finished I'll distill it all down to some basic guidelines you can apply so you'll feel confident that no matter what happens on the investment scene during your retirement years, you've done everything you can to make sure you'll have a reliable, worry-free income for the rest of your life.

The 40-Year Plan

If you retire, let's say, at the age of 60, then a 40-year plan would be solid. It takes you past your life expectancy, adding an extra layer of safety. As it happens, the 40-year period from 1973 through 2012 provides a great example of the worst *and* the best of what can happen to investments through the market's many and sundry ups and downs. It is one of the two worst 40-year time frames in the modern financial era[10] for investors needing income from a portfolio—those investors did in fact have to weather a perfect financial storm. In fact, if you'd retired in 1973 you'd have started taking income in the worst back-to-back years the stock market has seen since the era of the Great Depression, 1931 to 1932.[11] By looking at what actually happened to each type of investment vehicle during those years, we can play Monday morning quarterback and see how you would have done if you'd had to weather those storms. Would you have been enjoying the beach on your 95th birthday, or passing out shopping carts at Walmart?

To keep the numbers manageable, let's examine what happens to a $100,000 investment. Many people like to live off the return on their investments and leave the principal alone, so let's see how much that return would have been. Since that strategy is often unrealistic, we'll also see what would have happened if you'd taken a 5.5% disbursement, adjusting for inflation each year—and find out how long your money would have lasted. We'll apply all these factors to the most common methods of investing for income:

- Certificates of deposit

- Treasury bills

- Long-term government bonds

- Long-term corporate bonds

- An S&P 500 index fund

---

10   The other is the 40-year period beginning in 1969.

11   Roger G. Ibbotson, "The Long-Run Perspective," *2020 SBBI Yearbook: Stocks, Bonds, Bills, and Inflation: US Capital Markets Performance by Asset Class 1926-2019*, 12-13.

- The Investment Company of America® fund[12]

In the end, we'll gather all the data and put together a portfolio that would indeed have survived that perfect financial storm, and left you more concerned about running out of sunscreen than money.

Certificates of Deposit

Certificates of deposit (CDs) are bank investments insured by the FDIC up to a certain limit, currently $250,000 per depositor, per bank (the rules change from time to time) for all the money you have in a given financial institution. They pay you a guaranteed return, for a specified length of time. Many retirees like CDs because once you buy the instrument, the interest rate doesn't fluctuate until they mature and you reinvest the cash in a new CD (or cash them out and hold the cash or invest the money in a different vehicle). Also, business risk (the risk that a company will go under) is virtually eliminated up to a certain amount because of the government backing through FDIC insurance.

How did CDs do during our 1973 to 2012 time frame? This was one of the *best* periods for fixed investments since the Great Depression. They were paying historically high rates in 1973; those rates soared to record highs in the late 1970s and stayed high through most of the 1980s. But by 2002 the rates had plummeted.

---

12 The Investment Company of America® is a mutual fund offered as one of the American Funds family of funds. It is listed here only as an example; the listing should not be considered a recommendation of the fund.

CERTIFICATES OF DEPOSIT[13] 1973 THROUGH 2012		
	Return	Year
Highest return	15.92%	1981
Lowest return	0.42%	2011
Average return	6.16%	

If you're one of those people who like to live off the interest from your investments, that strategy would have had devastating consequences here. In 1981, for every $100,000 you had invested in CDs you would have received $15,920 in interest. Not bad! But if you stuck to this strategy in 2011, you would have only received $420 in interest. Not a pretty picture. The problem is complicated in this case because CDs are fairly inflexible if you need more money than the interest rate provides. If you tap into the principal of a CD before it matures, you'll probably be charged a penalty.

For the purposes of our experiment, let's assume you bought a 6-month CD so that you could take your 5.5% disbursement even when interest rates fell below that level. (These are pretty unrealistic assumptions, but go with me here.) Let's run it through our financial gauntlet. We start with $100,000 and take out $5,500 at the beginning of year 1, and increase your income stream by the inflation rate every year.

Doing this, in one of the best time frames in history for CDs, your hypothetical CD ran out of money in year 24. Not bad, but keep in mind, these were the best of times for CDs. You can't find a 15.92% CD today. What's particularly striking is that even if you were to duplicate that banner era for CDs, if you want your income to last

---

13   Certificates of deposit with 6-month maturities.

for 40 years you'd only be able to take an initial distribution of 3.8%, or $3,800 a year—a substantial decrease from our target of 5.5%. If this is how CDs fare in the best of times (for this type of investment), can you imagine how they would do in bad times?

Treasury Bills

Treasury bills, or T-bills, are another favorite of those taking income, in part because the return of your investment at maturity is backed by the full faith and credit of the United States government. A T-bill is essentially a short-term loan to the government from the investor, much like a government bond. But unlike a bond, you can feel reasonably confident it will hold its value. Because T-bills mature in a short period of time, their value fluctuates very little. If you have to sell it before it matures, you might lose some of your original investment. But otherwise it performs much like cash in your portfolio. (This is why it's considered a cash investment rather than a fixed income investment.)

Our test period of 1973 to 2012 was a great time frame for T-bills. Like CDs, they posted record highs.

TREASURY BILLS 1973 THROUGH 2012		
	Return	Year
Highest return	14.71%	1981
Lowest return	0.04%	2011
Average return	5.37%	

To understand just how good our 40-year test period was for Treasury bills, consider that the average rate of return for this period was nearly 80% higher than the average rate of return during the 87 years from 1926 (when we started tracking them) through 2012—

5.37% compared to 3.1%. In fact, the highest 20-year period for T-bills since 1926 was 1972 to 1991. The low interest rates didn't kick in till the back end of our 40-year time frame. (Keep this in mind when you examine the numbers—we'll come back to it shortly.)

Even in this best-of-times scenario for T-bills, if you were living on interest alone you would have had a mere $40 a year to live on in 2011. **If you had drawn an initial distribution of $5,500 and adjusted for inflation each year, your T-bill portfolio would have lasted just 21 years in the best market for T-bills that history can offer.** If your goal is to have your money last for 40 years, you'd have to cut that initial annual distribution down to 3.15%, or just $3,150.

Long-Term Government Bonds

Long-term government bonds are like T-bills in that they are a loan to the government, but for a longer time frame. They usually pay higher interest rates, and have larger swings in their fair market value due to interest rate risk—remember, with any bond, when interest rates go up the value of bonds goes down (see Chapter Four, "Investments 101," under "Fixed Investments"). This is especially true of long-term bonds.

Like T-bills, the 1973 to 2012 time frame includes the all-time best 20-year period for long-term government bonds. That was 1982 to 2001, with an average return of 12.09% per year.

LONG-TERM GOVERNMENT BONDS 1973 THROUGH 2012		
	Return	Year
Highest return	40.36%	1982
Lowest return	-14.90%	2009
Average return	9.51%	

This is the first time you've seen the impact of risk on an income investor. For this time period, long-term government bonds had an average return that was almost 50% better than T-bills. However, remember our discussion about reverse dollar cost averaging—volatility can decrease the life expectancy of your money. As a result, **when tested during the time frame 1973 to 2012, long-term government bonds lasted only 17 years.** That's right, this portfolio was depleted 4 years sooner than your Treasury bills. The increase in volatility outweighed the higher returns, with severe consequences to how long your retirement income would last. To make your retirement fund last 40 years, you would have had to start out taking just 3.75%, or $3,750. This is more than you could have taken with the T-bills, which may be counterintuitive, since at the 5.5% distribution rate the long-term government bonds didn't last as long. The difference here is that your long-term government bonds had an outstanding performance in the initial years of our test period, but had a much higher volatility, which decreased the lifetime of their income stream.

Long-Term Corporate Bonds

Long-term corporate bonds are similar to government bonds in that they are loans for a set period of time, but they are loans from you to corporations. They generally pay a higher interest rate because there is a higher risk of default, or business risk—if the corporation falls on hard financial times, so does your investment.

Like the long-term government bonds, 1973 to 2012 includes the all-time best 20-year period for this type of investment—from 1982 through 2001 these bonds returned an average of 12.13% per year.

LONG-TERM CORPORATE BONDS 1973 THROUGH 2012		
	Return	Year
Highest return	42.56%	1982
Lowest return	-7.84%	1999
Average return	9.35%	

When tested during the time frame 1973 to 2012, with a 5.5% initial distribution, long-term corporate bonds lasted only 19 years. This is better than long-term government bonds, but not as good as T-bills. To have your fund last 40 years, your initial distribution would need to be 3.85%, or $3,850.

S&P 500 Index Fund

Our CDs and bonds haven't fared very well in our perfect financial storm, but what about the stock market? Might equity investments provide a stream of income that will last throughout your retirement years?

One way to test this is to look at a mutual fund that represents a cross section of equities. (We'll talk more about mutual funds in Chapter Eleven, "The Best Way to (Mutual) Fund Your All-Weather Retirement Portfolio," starting on page 139.) Index funds are a class of investments that do just that—they're a collection of stocks that tries to mirror a common index like the Dow Jones or Standard & Poor's 500, commonly called the S&P 500. These are popular funds because they're seen by many as good performers. In fact, you may have heard something like, "Most mutual fund managers can't beat the index, so you should just invest in an index fund."

One of the most popular indexes is the S&P 500. It consists of five hundred stocks that are a representative sample of the entire market, designed to track the activity of the market as a whole. Among the biggest S&P 500 funds is the one offered by Vanguard, one of the largest and most respected investment firms. Because it costs money to manage any mutual fund, those expenses will be deducted from the return paid to investors, so the actual return of an index fund will usually be slightly less than the performance of the index itself.

For simplicity's sake, though, let's use the S&P 500 itself to generate our test numbers for 1973 through 2012. The period started out brutally for stocks (and their indexes), with the worst back-to-back years since the Great Depression, and this index reflects that.

S&P 500 1973 THROUGH 2012		
	Return	Year
Highest return	37.47%	1995
Lowest return	-38.47%	2008
Average return	8.00%	

During the 1973 to 2012 time frame, the S&P 500 posted a nice average return for the time period. **Still, if you test it using our criteria, taking a 5.5% disbursement at the beginning of year 1 and increasing the amount by the actual inflation rate, the S&P 500 lasts just 12 years.** And you'd only be able to take an initial distribution of 2.6%, or $2,600, if your goal is to have your investment fund last 40 years.

Investment Company of America® Fund

Some say you should find a mutual fund with a long and impressive track record. The Investment Company of America (ICA) fund, offered by the American Funds family of mutual funds, does in fact have a long and impressive track record. This fund was started before the Great Depression and is still around today. Not many funds have that kind of longevity. Many of the people I know in the industry recommend this fund to their clients. One well-respected advisor told me it's the greatest fund in history. That's debatable, but it certainly has performed well in the past.

Historically, the ICA fund has been a front-end loaded fund— that means you pay a sales charge when you buy into it. Typically the load starts at 5.75% for small investments (under $25,000) and goes away if you have $1,000,000 or more.

Okay, so let's put it through our financial gauntlet. For our purposes here, we've used our standard $100,000 initial investment and deducted 3.5%, the actual sales charge for that amount ($100,000) up front. Remember, our test period starts out during some of the worst times in the history of the market.

ICA Fund 1973 THROUGH 2012[14]		
	Return	Year
Highest return	27.67%	1975
Lowest return	-34.7%	2008
Average return	6.74%	

As good as it is, when we run the ICA Fund through this perfect financial storm, we find it lasted just 20 years. Even though this mutual fund is a good one on its own, if you need income for 40 years, 20 years simply won't cut it. That said, as individual mutual

---

14   Information supplied to me by American Funds about the performance of the Investment Company of America™ Fund, Class A shares, during this time frame. Charges may vary depending on a variety of factors, including, but not limited to, amount invested in the fund, amount invested in other American Funds, and so forth.

funds go, this is actually one of the better ones out there. Twenty years of income is more than most individual funds can offer, but it's certainly not good enough to provide you with a secure income for the rest of your life—even if you retire when you're 60 and live only as long as the life expectancy tables say you will. If you live longer … clearly this plan just isn't good enough.

Bottom line, finding one mutual fund with a long and impressive track record still won't give you the lifelong income you're looking for. To have your investment fund last 40 years, even with this top performer, you would have to start out with an annual distribution of 4.65%, or $4,650. We can do better.

Summary

I've put together a snapshot of each of the investments we've discussed in this chapter, with an analysis of 1) how long your income would last with an initial 5.5% distribution, and 2) the initial distribution rate you could take if you want your income stream to last 40 years. Here's a summary of what we have so far:

	HOW LONG YOUR MONEY WOULD LAST	YOUR INITIAL DISTRIBUTION FOR 40 YEARS OF INCOME
CDs	24 years	3.80%
T-bills	21 years	3.15%
Long-term government bonds	17 years	3.75%
Long-term corporate bonds	19 years	3.85%
S&P 500	12 years	2.60%
ICA fund	20 years	4.65%

So what have we discovered?

- Common methods for investing for income simply don't work in the financial storm scenario.

- Guaranteed cash investments, like Treasury bills, can't generate sustained income throughout the retirement years.

- Fixed investments, like long-term CDs or bonds, fall short even in good times.

- Equity investments, like stocks, also fall short, even though they had high average returns over our 40-year test period.

- One of the top mutual funds falls short. This would indicate that picking great funds, even with wonderful hindsight, is not good enough.

A Portfolio That Can Weather the Storm

Okay, I know what you're thinking. So far, every one of the investments we've looked at has failed the test, with even the best performers unable to provide income for much more than half of our projected retirement years. Does that mean you're sailing on a sinking ship? Not at all. There is in fact a ship that can weather the storm. Its name, my friend, is *Diversification*.

Placing your money in a carefully chosen array of diverse investment areas—stocks in large companies and small companies, government bonds, corporate bonds, and so forth—is the key to having a worry-free income for life. When you choose a variety of investments that have dissimilar movements in various economic scenarios—that is, when one investment goes down another is going up—you protect yourself no matter what kind of storm looms on the economic horizon.

To get a sense of why diversification is so powerful, and how differently these various investment vehicles perform at a given time, take a look at the following grids. Compare the best years, worst years, and average returns for the bonds versus stocks, small versus large, and so on. First, here's how they compare for the 94-year period from 1926 through 2019:

94-YEAR COMPARISON			
	Average Return[15]	Best Year/ Return	Worst Year/ Return	Number of years investment had a positive return
Stocks: large company	12.1%	1933 53.99%	1931 -43.34%	69
Stocks: small company	16.3%	1933 142.87%	1937 -58.01%	65
Long-term corporate bonds	6.4%	1982 42.56%	1969 -8.09%	74
Long-term government bonds	6.0%	1982 40.36%	2009 -14.9%	69
US Treasury bills	3.4%	1981 14.71%	1938 -0.02%	93

There is no such thing as a perfect investment. If you were entirely in large company stocks in 1931 your "portfolio" went down 43.34%. If you were in long-term government bonds, your portfolio lost 14.9% in 2009. However, even with a basic diversified portfolio of ⅓ large company stocks, ⅓ long-term government bonds, and ⅓

---

15   Arithmetic annualized return.

Treasury bills, this simple diversified portfolio lost 20.67% in 1931, and gained 2.9% in 2009. A substantial improvement.

Now, let's look at how those same investment areas fared during a perfect financial storm time period, from 1973 through 2012:

40-YEAR (PERFECT FINANCIAL STORM) COMPARISON[16]			
	Average Return[17]	Best Year/ Return	Worst Year/ Return	Number of years investment had a positive return
Stocks: large company	11.38%	1995 37.43%	2008 -37.00%	31
Stocks: small company	15.31%	1976 57.38%	2008 -36.72%	29
Long-term corporate bonds	9.35%	1982 42.56%	1999 -7.45%	32
Long-term government bonds	9.51%	1982 40.36%	2009 -14.9%	30
US Treasury bills	5.37%	1981 14.71%	2011 0.04%	40

You can see why a properly diversified portfolio, with different elements moving in different directions at any given time, creates a balance that will outlast any one of its components through virtually any financial storm.

But how do you diversify? How much money do you put into each asset class? Where can you go for information? Has there been

---

16   Roger G. Ibbotson, "The Long-Run Perspective," *2020 SBBI Yearbook: Stocks, Bonds, Bills, and Inflation: US Capital Markets Performance by Asset Class 1926-2019*, 12-13.

17   Arithmetic annualized return.

research in this area? Of course there has. But what research do you trust, and where do you find it? Not only that, do you really want to spend years sifting through the research? Probably not—and you won't need to.

In the coming chapters you'll find an investment strategy that's sane and sensible, and a step-by-step guide to creating a portfolio designed to survive a perfect financial storm like the one we've analyzed here or any of the others we've seen since 1930. I'll show you how to build such a portfolio for yourself, as well as a simple "8-Year Rule" that will add an even greater level of protection. With those strategies in place, you'll be ready to sail off into the sunset knowing you've done everything a wise investor can do to create a worry-free income for life.

PART III.

Designing Your All-Weather Retirement Portfolio

Chapter Eight

The Two Most Important Questions

H ave you ever wondered why the experts so often disagree about investment strategies? It seems there are as many opinions about where to put your money, and when to put it there, as there are talking heads on TV. Even among highly trained, experienced analysts, you're likely to find vastly different recommendations.

For the most part, the broad variation in viewpoints comes down to differences in philosophy about investing, about what works and what doesn't. Like anything else in life, the decisions we make about financial matters reflect our views about how the world operates. When it comes to your investments, your own personal philosophy depends on how you answer two simple questions:

1. **Can I time the market?** That is, can I reliably "buy low and sell high"? Is it possible to anticipate market movements and interest rates before the other so-called market timing experts?

2. **Can I spot the hot investments?** If I do my homework—study the literature, read my *Wall Street Journal* every day, scrutinize financial statements and prospectuses—will I be able to identify those opportunities that are about to take off?

> Like anything else in life, the decisions we make about financial matters reflect our views about how the world operates.

These two questions are more important than any other you will ask about investing. How you answer them will determine your investment philosophy—and quite likely the course of your financial future.

Two Questions = *Four Investment Strategies*

Given that each of these two questions has two possible answers—yes or no—it's possible to arrive at four different strategies based on your answers:

1. You *can* time the market, and you *can* pick hot investments.

2. You *can't* time the market, but you *can* pick hot investments.

3. You *can* time the market, but *can't* pick hot investments.

4. You *can't* time the market, and you *can't* you pick hot investments.

Roger Gibson, author of the widely acclaimed book *Asset Allocation: Balancing Financial Risk*, uses this approach to identify four different investment styles: the Guru, the Analyst, the Market Timer, and the Prudent Long-Term Investor. He sorts them into the following matrix:

WHAT KIND OF INVESTOR ARE YOU?			
		Can you time the market?	
		Yes	No
Can you pick the hot investments?	Yes	1. A Guru	2. An Analyst
	No	3. A Market Timer	4. A Prudent Long-Term Investor

Investment Style #1: The Guru

If you believe you can spot market trends as well as hot investment opportunities, you're a market Guru. These investors (or advisors) believe in both market timing and superior investment selection. They try to stay ahead of the pack in finding undervalued stocks that will deliver market-beating returns. In addition, these investors believe it is possible to identify the mispricing of an entire market sector and predict when it will turn up or down. In other words, they believe they can time the market. You often find would-be "crystal-ball readers" from the media in this category, forecasters who profess to be able to predict what the market will do in the days, weeks, or hours to come.

Investment Style #2: The Analyst

If you're an Analyst, you don't believe you can predict market swings consistently with any degree of accuracy. However, you do believe that with careful market analysis you can uncover undervalued investments and deliver market-beating returns. Many professional portfolio managers rely on their ability to scrutinize the data to identify the next rising star before the rest of the market catches on and drives the price skyward. This is the approach I learned in graduate school. Many stockbrokers and money managers use this approach.

Investment Style #3: The Market Timer

If you believe in spotting trends, but don't put much faith in analyzing individual investment vehicles, you're a Market Timer. You're the kind of investor who watches the bigger picture in hopes of buying at the bottom of the market (or near it) and selling at the top.

Regarding advisors and market timing, it is my belief that advisors add much more value when they protect a client from the impulse to buy or sell out of greed or fear than they ever could by trying to squeeze an extra 1% return by trying to time the market.

Investment Style #4: The Prudent Long-Term Investor

If you're a Prudent Long-Term Investor, chances are you believe that nobody can predict the future. You also probably feel it's extremely difficult to beat the thousands of astute money managers who are trying to outperform the market (and each other). Instead, you use an approach we call *asset allocation*. You avoid putting all your eggs in one basket by putting your money in a variety of investment vehicles. You diversify among cash, fixed, and equity investments, and diversify further into different types of assets within each category.

Why is diversification the mark of a "prudent" long-term investor? Remember that different types of investments perform differently in any given economic scenario. By putting your eggs in lots of different baskets, you reduce your risk of taking a debilitating hit should the bottom fall out of one sector of the economy. Approximately 60% of pension plans, endowments, and similar institutional portfolios are managed according to this principle.

Testing the Investment Styles

So how do we test the validity of these investment styles, and determine which is best for you? Simple. We look at the arguments of those who advocate them.

Investors in the first three styles share one very important philosophical belief: They believe it is possible to consistently uncover undervalued stocks and bonds—that is, those that are priced lower than the true value of the companies or government entities they represent—then buy low and sell high to generate an exceptional return for the portfolio. Most importantly, these investors believe they can do it better than other advisors or money managers, time after time after time.

Prudent Long-Term Investors, on the other hand, respect the ability of the market to generate prices that are realistic and appropriate—over time, if not on a day-to-day basis. They seek to capture solid returns by allocating funds in such a way that a portfolio can draw on the strength of one market segment or another, no matter what's going on in the economic world at large.

Whatever your investment style is—whether you trust the ability of the market to generate appropriate prices or not—your basic goal is to generate reasonable returns and minimize risk. Testing the effectiveness of the investment style, then, is fundamentally a risk versus return problem. We can look at the track records of professional investors who embrace each of our four styles and see how they've fared. If the Guru, Analyst, Market Timer, or Prudent Long-Term Investor add value, this value should be reflected in their returns, and we should expect to see the same managers on top over and over again. We can also look at independent research that measures risk and return within each different approach to get some hard numbers that separate expectations from real results.

Since the Guru, the Market Timer, and the Analyst have so much in common, let's look at those first. Most mutual fund managers fall into one of these categories—they all believe they can use their expertise to beat the market. If one style or another were truly effective, we would see certain managers consistently producing the best returns. I've scrutinized data from Morningstar, the premier independent rating service for stocks, bonds, and mutual funds, and found that such shining stars are few and far between. In general, the top managers—and their funds—in any given year fail to rise to the top in subsequent years. What's more, less than half of these professionally managed funds outperform the market in any given year.

To be fair to the Guru, the Market Timer, and the Analyst, the fact that we don't see repeatable excellence does not mean these approaches are entirely without merit. There have been excellent active managers who have clearly added substantial value. Warren Buffett and Peter Lynch are examples of investment professionals who have consistently done just that. But these two men are legendary precisely because of their unique accomplishments. Examples of similar track records are very limited, and the performances of most managers fall within the parameters we'd expect from a random statistical sample.

What are the odds you'll be able to do better? And what are the odds you'll find a money manager who is the next Warren Buffett or Peter Lynch? Are you willing to bet your retirement on it?

Investment styles #1 through #3 are enticing to investors because of the emotional dialogue. To investors, this dialogue is the siren song of quick wealth, return without risk, or secret information: "Trust us, we will find you great wealth and prosperity." Or, "Trust us and we will show you how to beat the market with what we know." Of course, you and I know that for every successful explorer who found untold wealth in the New World, a thousand others failed. It seems to me that investment styles #1, #2, and #3 speak to investors who want short-term gratification at the expense of long-term, worry-free income for life.

Your Personal Investment Style for a Worry-Free Income for Life

So now we can answer the question, "How should I invest to provide a worry-free income for life?"

The answer: Investment style #4. Be a prudent long-term investor. Period.

Why do I believe so passionately in this strategy? Applying the principles of asset allocation allows you (or your advisor) to spend your time implementing time-tested investment solutions without relying on the guessing games of market timing and picking individual stocks. Time is spent on what really matters: how to diversify and find the mutual funds that will consistently deliver a performance consistent with their asset classes.

Some call this approach boring. "Old school." Maybe so. I certainly don't make any claims that it's a "get rich quick" or a return-without-risk strategy. Rather, as a Prudent Long-Term Investor your expectations will be substantially more modest than

> If you stay invested, you will receive good, reasonable returns for the given level of risk. You will maximize the probability that you will have a worry-free income for the rest of your life, no matter what kind of financial storm occurs in the world around you.

that. If you stay invested, you will receive good, reasonable returns for the given level of risk. You will maximize the probability that you will have a worry-free income for the rest of your life, no matter what kind of financial storm occurs in the world around you.

Turn the page, and together we'll walk through the ten steps you can take to create that worry-free portfolio.

Chapter Nine

Ten Steps to a Worry-Free Income for Life

We've settled on an investment style that's prudent and practical, one that gives you the best probability that, no matter what happens in the outside world, you'll have a worry-free income for life. We've agreed that asset allocation will provide the best balance of return and risk, while protecting you from the potential financial storms coming your way.

The principles are sound. Now how do we put them into practice? How do you allocate your assets among the mind-boggling array of investments options available? How do you design a portfolio that will allow you to enjoy your retirement with the peace of mind that comes from *knowing* you've done all you can do to ensure a solid financial future?

This chapter is the key to making it a reality. I'll take you step by step through the process of moving money into different types of investments so you'll have a properly diversified portfolio—a true All-

Weather Retirement Portfolio. At each step—there will be ten in all—we'll evaluate how the portfolio would have performed by running it through the Perfect Financial Storm (PFS) Test. That means we'll test it against every 40-year time frame since 1930, the first year for which we have the necessary market data. While past performance doesn't guarantee future results, analyzing a full 90 years of historical data gives us a solid foundation to stand on when we evaluate the various diversification strategies we'll apply in each of the ten steps.

Our goal is to see how the portfolio would have performed in every scenario—when the investment markets performed well for an investor drawing an income, like you, and when they performed miserably because the markets delivered a perfect financial storm. As it happens, 1937 and 1969 were the worst years in our 90-year test period for people in the early years of their retirement—that's when investors like you experienced a true perfect financial storm. As we go through the steps of building your All-Weather Retirement Portfolio and applying the Perfect Financial Storm Test, you'll see how those events affected the performance of the portfolio.

> Remember, this is all about showing you how you can have a worry-free income for life. You'll see—it's much easier than you think.

Why go to all that trouble? Because we want you to be able to enjoy your retirement with the confidence in knowing your money is invested using an approach that has withstood the test of time. Remember, this is all about showing you how you can have a worry-free income for life.

You'll see—it's much easier than you think.

The All-Weather Retirement Portfolio

First, let's define our goals, so we're clear about what the All-Weather Retirement Portfolio should do for you:

1. The ideal portfolio will provide you an annual spendable cash flow of 5.5% of its initial value.

2. Your income will be protected from inflation, because you'll adjust your disbursement each year at a rate equivalent to the rate of inflation. Exceptions will be applied only when the worst perfect financial storms strike. (Don't worry—that's a rare event. In all the 40-year time frames we studied, the exception applied just 4% of the time.)

3. It should weather all financial storms—including those perfect financial storms that can be so devastating for a retiree like yourself—and provide you with a worry-free income for 40 years.

Next, we'll apply the Perfect Financial Storm Test to assess how well our All-Weather Retirement Portfolio would have performed against all these criteria. Here's how it works:

*   Let's assume the portfolio has a starting value of $100,000.

*   We'll withdraw the annual distribution at the beginning of each year,[18] starting with an inflation-protected initial distribution rate of 5.5%. For example, in year one we'll pull out $5,500 on January 1.

*   We'll build the portfolio one step at a time, diversifying your investments as we go. With each step we will look at how

---

18   As you'll see on page 199 in Chapter Thirteen, "Make Your All-Weather Retirement Portfolio Even Sunnier," I recommend you take your distributions monthly. Unfortunately, the data I used for the PFS Test are only available on an annual basis, so I used an annual distribution for our purposes here.

the portfolio would have performed through every single rolling 40-year time frame from 1930 to 2019. (There are 51 of them.)

- In each step we'll look at the portfolio's success rate. This is a measure of how many times in our 90-year test period the portfolio lasted the full 40 years without being depleted, while providing an inflation-protected initial distribution of 5.5%. The higher the success rate, the better.

- In each step I'll show you how long your money would have lasted—or, put another way, how long it would have taken for your portfolio to be depleted—in the worst 40-year time frame in our 90-year test period. Remember, our baseline criteria demand that your portfolio will provide you with a worry-free income for 40 years, so that's our target here. Nothing less will do.[19]

Sound like tough criteria for success? Well, it is. But the stakes are too high to shoot for anything less. As we've seen in earlier chapters, many of the ways people commonly invest for retirement fall short. Some of those would succeed if everything in the economy happens to go just right. But what you need is an approach that has the best possible chance of succeeding no matter what the economy does. If you build your portfolio around the ten key steps that follow, you shall have it.

---

19   For a more in-depth look, including analyses for 30- and 35-year rolling time frames as well as 95% and 100% successful distribution rates, go to www.TheRetirement-Path.com and click on "Resources," then "Helpful Articles."

Step One: Use Intermediate-Term Corporate Bonds

Bonds are basically a loan you make to the government, a church, a corporation, or some other entity. That entity pays you a predetermined amount of interest in regular payments (usually semi-annually) over a specified amount of time. The interest rate they pay depends on many factors, such as the level of credit risk you assume (that's the risk that the entity issuing the bond will default on the loan), the terms of payment, the length of time you'll hold the bond, and so forth. (For a more detailed discussion of bonds, refer back to Chapter Four, "Investments 101.")

Let's be clear: In terms of your return on your investment, bonds generally underperform relative to stocks over the long haul. Still, many people turn to them when they're looking for reliable investment income. The primary advantage of any individual bond is that if you hold it until it matures, you know exactly how much your investment will earn. If interest rates go down, you'll be glad you locked yours in at a favorable rate. However, if interest rates go up, you won't benefit from the increase until your bond matures and you can sell it and buy again at the higher rate; until then, you can't replace the bond with a new one without incurring an additional cost. The longer the term, the greater the risk that interest rates elsewhere will rise and your investment will lose value as a result. That's why longer-term bonds generally pay a higher rate than their short-term cousins.

There's also a risk that the entity you've invested in can go bankrupt. That's highly unlikely with government bonds, but a real consideration if the issuer is a corporation or other private entity. There's some consolation in knowing that in a bankruptcy, bondholders are paid before stockholders, so there's a chance you'll get some, if not all, of your money back. And when you hold bonds within a mutual fund, your money is spread among hundreds or even thousands of bonds, so the impact of a single default on that portion of your portfolio is reduced significantly. (For much more on this topic, see Chapter Eleven, "The Best Way to (Mutual) Fund Your All-Weather Retirement Portfolio," starting on page 139.) Still, the risk is real.

So why should you buy bonds at all?

Because in many economic circumstances, they move differently from stocks. That is, when stocks do well, bonds generally don't. But when stocks plummet, bonds are generally strong. This is what you want, because it gives you stability in the face of that perfect financial storm.

Many experts recommend using long-term government bonds because they generally offer a higher yield than intermediate-term bonds, and because government bonds in general carry no credit risk. Based on my experience and extensive analysis of the data since 1930, I find intermediate-term corporate bonds, which have a maturity of around 5 to 8 years, to be the best choice for your retirement portfolio.

Let's look at their track record.

If you buy bonds, what can you expect to earn from your investment? Let's examine how intermediate-term bonds from US corporations performed across the 90-year period from 1930 through 2019.

- The average return[20] was 5.72%.

- The best year was 1982, with a return of 31.30%.

- The worst year was 1945, with a -4.43% return.

- Out of 90 years, 77 were positive.

- The best ten-year time frame was 1982 through 1991, with an annual return of 13.99%.

---

20   Arithmetic annualized return.

- The worst ten-year time frame was 1940 through 1949, with an annual return of 1.25%.

- Out of 81 ten-year time frames, 81 were positive.[21]

Put it to the test.

Now let's look at how our intermediate-term corporate bonds would do in our perfect financial storm, the yearly economic ups and downs that occurred in each 40-year time frame from 1930 through 2019. We'll call it our Perfect Financial Storm Test, or the PFS Test. The following table gives us all the details.

THE PERFECT FINANCIAL STORM TEST: STEP ONE ($100,000 initial portfolio with a 5.5% inflation-protected annual distribution, tested against every 40-year time frame since 1930)			
WILL YOUR MONEY LAST 40 YEARS?			
	Success Rate	Shortest Time to Depletion in 100% of Cases Tested*	Shortest Time to Depletion in 96% of Cases Tested**
Step One: Intermediate-term corporate bonds	2%	14 years	14 years
*Includes every 40-year time frame since 1930. **Does not include 40-year time frames starting in 1937 and 1969.			

Here are some key points regarding intermediate-term corporate bonds:

- Our "success rate" is just 2%. In other words, in 2% of the 40-year time frames we tested, our bonds met our target of

---

21   GlobalFinancialData.com. The intermediate corporate bond data series is a syn-thesized data series derived from long-term government bonds, intermediate-term government bonds, and long-term corporate bonds.

lasting 40 years before our investment was depleted. That includes applying our basic ground rules, taking an initial 5.5% disbursement and bumping it by the inflation rate every year.

- When we looked at each of the fifty-one 40-year time frames in our test period, the shortest amount of time it took for our investment to be depleted was just 14 years—and that's true even when we exclude the worst years to begin your retirement, 1937 and 1969.

The bottom line is this: With bonds alone, the portfolio fails the PFS Test, because it doesn't meet our basic parameter: It doesn't last 40 years.

No worries. That's why we have nine more steps. Read on.

Step Two: Diversify with Stocks for a Higher Return

Stocks are sometimes called equity or ownership assets because when you own a stock, you actually own part of the company. Maybe you own a very small part of the company, but you still own it. And hopefully your stock will increase in value so you build equity. Equity assets tend to outperform debt investments (such as bonds) over time. They also have more risk. (For more detailed information about stocks, see Chapter Four, "Investments 101.")

One of the risks in owning stocks is the possibility that the company will fail, and after paying the money owed to bondholders there will be nothing left for stockholders. A critical concern is that when you hold a large portion of your wealth in a few stocks and one goes under, your personal loss can be severe. Does Enron, Lehman Brothers, Circuit City, or Borders ring a bell? This is called *business risk* and can be virtually eliminated through proper diversification through mutual funds.

Even if the company doesn't go under, the value of your stocks could go down, and it's a very real risk to your portfolio and your future. In fact, you should understand that, historically, usually in 3 years out of 10 the stock market has gone down. No one has ever been able to accurately predict when market downturns will happen (and I can assure you, I won't be the first). This is the price you pay for a greater return over time. Keep in mind that when a down year happens, you *can* weather the storm. Just don't set yourself up for failure. Recognize that there will be down years, and put yourself in a position to ride them out. The portfolio we're creating in this chapter is designed to do just that.

But with so much potential for stormy weather, why include stocks at all?

Two reasons. First, over the long term, and with sound planning, stocks are likely to generate a greater return than bonds or, for that matter, better than most any other type of investment. Second—and this is critical—remember that in any given economic scenario, equity assets tend to move differently from bonds. Again, this is exactly what you want. When one portion of your portfolio suffers, another portion is likely to be thriving. Think of it as a lifeboat in that perfect storm—one that floats even when other ships are sinking.

Let's look at their track record.

As we know, stocks usually have a higher return than bonds in the long run. Let's see how they did during the 90 years from 1930 through 2019. To keep things simple, we'll look only at stocks of large United States corporations.

- The average annual return[22] was 11.69%.

- The best year was 1933, with a return of 53.99%.

---

22 Arithmetic annualized return.

- The worst year was 1931 (no surprise there), with a -43.34% return. (2008 came in second, with a loss of 37.00%.)

- Out of 90 years, 67 were positive. It's interesting to note here that, when you adjust for inflation, 61 years out of 90 were positive.

- The best ten-year time frame was 1949 through 1958, with an annual return of 20.06%.

- The worst ten-year time frame was 1999 to 2008, with an annual return of -1.38%.

- Out of 81 ten-year time frames, 78 were positive.[23]

So far, so good. Clearly, these stocks did better than the bonds we looked at in Step One. But remember the impact of volatility and reverse dollar cost averaging in a volatile market. (If you need a refresher, turn back to Chapter Five, "Investing for Income Is Different.") By keeping a portion of our portfolio in bonds, we'll offset some of that volatility. That's the power of diversification. To apply that principle here, we'll put 60% of the portfolio in stocks from large US companies, but we'll keep 40% in our intermediate-term corporate bonds. Here's what it looks like:

Put it to the test.

Will that strategy meet your needs? In other words, does it pass our PFS Test, and provide an income that lasts 40 years?

In a word, no. However, it is a nice improvement over Step One, when the entire portfolio was in intermediate-term corporate bonds. Stocks will be the cornerstone of the portfolio that protects you against a bad inflationary time frame. The 60/40 ratio gives you a nice balance

---

23   Roger G. Ibbotson, *2020 SBBI Yearbook: US Capital Markets Performance by Asset Class 1926-2019*, Duff & Phelps (New York), 2.12-2.19.

between the high return offered by stocks and the reduced volatility of bonds. Here's what our portfolio looks like:

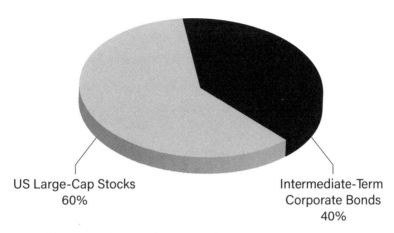

STEP TWO
DIVERSIFY WITH STOCKS & BONDS

US Large-Cap Stocks
60%

Intermediate-Term
Corporate Bonds
40%

And here are the numbers at a glance:

THE PERFECT FINANCIAL STORM TEST: STEP TWO ($100,000 initial portfolio with a 5.5% inflation-protected annual distribution, tested against every 40-year time frame since 1930)			
WILL YOUR MONEY LAST 40 YEARS?			
	Success Rate	Shortest Time to Depletion in 100% of Cases Tested*	Shortest Time to Depletion in 96% of Cases Tested**
Step One: Intermediate-term corporate bonds	2%	14 years	14 years
Step Two: US stocks, large companies	45%	17 years	18 years
*Includes every 40-year time frame since 1930. **Does not include 40-year time frames starting in 1937 and 1969.			

Our success rate for meeting our goal of having the portfolio last 40 years has increased dramatically—from 2%, when the portfolio contained only bonds, to 45%, when we add stocks. In other words, when we tested every 40-year time frame between 1930 and 2019, we met our goal 45% of the time. That includes taking an initial distribution of 5.5%, and increasing it by the amount of inflation each year.

Of the remaining time frames, the shortest amount of time it took for the portfolio to be depleted was 17 years. But now we start to see the impact of starting retirement in the midst of a perfect financial storm, like the ones we saw in 1937 and 1969. When we eliminate those years from our analysis, the shortest time to depletion is 18 years.

Step Three: Diversify Stocks Internationally

Now let's take a closer look at the equity side of our portfolio. Keep in mind that we're looking for investment classes that have dissimilar movements in any given economic situation. An obvious way to find them is, once again, to avoid putting all our eggs in one basket—or in one country. As we've seen, the economic climate affects the performance of your investments, and often the climate in the United States is different from that in other parts of the globe. That means that equities of companies based in Europe or Asia, for example, often perform differently from those of US corporations.

Some people hate to add international stocks. Why put your money into companies outside of the United States? Others are skeptical because in the 1990s international markets didn't perform as well as the US market. But you also have years like 1977, when the large US companies took a beating, going down more than 7%, while international companies went up more than 19%. It pays to diversify internationally. And that's my point. Historically, international markets and US stocks have moved differently in a given economic moment. Once again, this is what you're after. For this reason, I strongly believe that prudent investors, and certainly investors taking income, should diversify into the international markets.

Let's look at their track record.

Let's see how international stocks performed during the 90 years from 1930 through 2019.

- The average return[24] was 10.5%.

- The best year was 1933, with a return of 80.14%.

- The worst year was 2008, with a -43.20% return.

- Out of 90 years, 63 were positive.

- The best ten-year time frame was 1978 through 1987, with an annual return of 23.8%.

- The worst ten-year time frame was 1943 through 1952, with an annual return of 2.3%.

- Out of 81 ten-year time frames, 81 were positive.[25]

As you can see, there's a lot of data that suggest international stocks will make a worthwhile contribution to your portfolio. But how much of the portfolio should be moved into that asset class? There are a few studies that suggest the optimum level of international equities is as high as 50% of the stock portion of the portfolio. My own research and my experience (and my comfort level) are more aligned with the majority of studies, which recommend 30%.

---

24   Arithmetic annualized return.

25   GlobalFinancialData.com.

So, let's put 30% of your stocks in the international market. Since your stocks make up 60% of your total portfolio, that means your international stocks will account for 18% of your total portfolio, with 42% in US equities and 40% still in intermediate-term bonds. It'll look something like this:

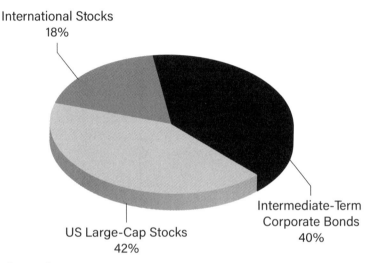

STEP THREE
DIVERSIFY STOCKS INTERNATIONALLY

International Stocks
18%

Intermediate-Term
Corporate Bonds
40%

US Large-Cap Stocks
42%

Put it to the test.

With this change we see a small but significant improvement in the life of our portfolio.

THE PERFECT FINANCIAL STORM TEST: STEP THREE
($100,000 initial portfolio with a 5.5% inflation-protected annual
distribution, tested against every 40-year time frame since 1930)

WILL YOUR MONEY LAST 40 YEARS?

	Success Rate	Shortest Time to Depletion in 100% of Cases Tested*	Shortest Time to Depletion in 96% of Cases Tested**
Step One: Intermediate-term corporate bonds	2%	14 years	14 years
Step Two: US stocks, large companies	45%	17 years	18 years
Step Three: International stocks	37%	19 years	19 years

*Includes every 40-year time frame since 1930.
**Does not include 40-year time frames starting in 1937 and 1969.

When we diversify with international stocks, we see an interesting shift in our PFS Test results. Our success rate drops to 37%, but we see an improvement in stability with the shortest time to depletion increasing to 19 years—even when we include those time frames starting in 1937 and 1969.

We'll see more evidence of the benefits of diversifying with international stocks as we continue to build our portfolio.

Step Four: Diversify with Growth and Value Stocks

Next, let's turn to some academic research. An important study by Kenneth French and Eugene Fama appeared in the June 1992 *Journal of Finance.*[26] It's just as valuable today as when it first came out. Their research revealed three "factors," or areas, that track dissimilar movements in the market, and how those factors affect the equity portion of your portfolio. If you diversify your investments according to these factors, you insulate yourself against loss in any one segment of the market. The three factors are:

1. Market risk: How much of your portfolio is in the stocks and how much is in bonds? If you put every dime you have in the stock market, and the market tanks, so will you. We took this factor into account early on when we decided not to put all your money into stocks, and included bonds in the portfolio.

2. Growth companies versus value companies: Basically, growth companies are companies whose profits are expected to grow rapidly. These usually don't pay a dividend because they want to plow their profits back into the business so the company will continue to grow. Because of their growth, investors usually find them exciting to own. Think Microsoft in the early years. Or Google. On the other hand, value stocks are often considered rather dull, like a ball-bearing manufacturer (*Yawn* ...). These stocks usually pay a high dividend, but earnings are expected to grow slowly. Sometimes value stocks are in favor and do well, sometimes it's growth. Sometimes both (and occasionally neither). We'll apply these principles here in Step Four.

3. Size—that is, large companies versus small companies, also known as "large-cap" and "small-cap" stocks: We usually take the largest 25% of the companies on the New York Stock

---

26   Eugene F. Fama and Kenneth R. French, "The Cross Section of Expected Stock Returns," *Journal of Finance* (June 1992), 427-465.

Exchange and call them "large," and call the smallest 25% "small." Certain economic climates favor large companies, while other climates favor small companies. You'll see how we apply this factor in Step Five.

When the stocks you own reflect a balanced selection of stocks within each of these factors, they create an "efficient" portfolio—one that provides the best expected return for a given level of volatility, or risk.

Let's look at their track record.

Here's how growth and value stocks performed from 1930 through 2019.

The average return[27] was:

- Large-cap growth: 11.32%

- Large-cap value: 14.92%

Out of 90 years, the number of positive years was:

- Large-cap growth: 68 years

- Large-cap value: 64 years

The best year was:

- Large-cap growth: 1954 at 47.33%

- Large-cap value: 1954 at 77.34%

The worst year was:

- Large-cap growth: 1931 at -36.12%

- Large-cap value: 1931 at -55.69%

The best decade:

- Large-cap growth: The 1990s, with an annual return of 20.1%.

---

27   Arithmetic annualized return.

- Large-cap value: The 1980s, with an annual return of 20.5%.

- The worst decade for large-cap growth stocks was the 2000s, with an annual return of -1.2%.

- The worst decade for large-cap value stocks was the 1930s, with an annual return of -4.5%.[28]

We'll start by diversifying the domestic (US) portion of your equities between 50% growth and 50% value stocks. That way you'll get the benefit of these two types of investments, and generate a balance between fluctuations in these two segments of the market. Let's see how our portfolio looks with that diversification in place:

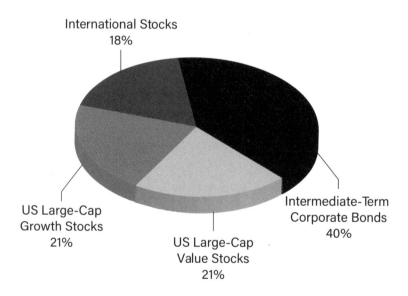

STEP FOUR
DIVERSIFY WITH GROWTH & VALUE

International Stocks
18%

US Large-Cap
Growth Stocks
21%

US Large-Cap
Value Stocks
21%

Intermediate-Term
Corporate Bonds
40%

---

28   Ibbotson, *2020 SBBI Yearbook*, 8.6-8.7.

Put it to the test.

And here's how it performs in our Perfect Financial Storm Test:

THE PERFECT FINANCIAL STORM TEST: STEP FOUR ($100,000 initial portfolio with a 5.5% inflation-protected annual distribution, tested against every 40-year time frame since 1930)			
WILL YOUR MONEY LAST 40 YEARS?			
	Success Rate	Shortest Time to Depletion in 100% of Cases Tested*	Shortest Time to Depletion in 96% of Cases Tested**
Step One: Intermediate-term corporate bonds	2%	14 years	14 years
Step Two: US stocks, large companies	45%	17 years	18 years
Step Three: International stocks	37%	19 years	19 years
Step Four: US stocks, growth & value	53%	20 years	22 years
*Includes every 40-year time frame since 1930. **Does not include 40-year time frames starting in 1937 and 1969.			

We've made good progress this time, with improvement in our success rate as well as the shortest time to depletion. Remember, though, it's not just this step that makes the difference, but the interplay between this and all that came before. Let's continue, and see what it takes to get to a portfolio that lasts 40 years 100% of the time.

Step Five: Diversify with Small Companies

The next step is to diversify the domestic (US) equity portion of the portfolio by splitting our large-cap US stocks into both large and small companies. We'll apply that strategy to both the growth and value segments of our portfolio.

Let's look at their track record.

Let's look at the time frame from 1930 through 2019 to get a sense of how each group has performed historically.

The average annual rate of return:[29]

- Small-cap growth: 13.2%

- Small-cap value: 18.8%

Out of 90 years, the number of positive years:

- Small-cap growth: 59 years

- Small-cap value: 65 years

The best year:

- Small-cap growth: 1933 at 149.39%

- Small-cap value: 1933 at 132.81%

The worst year:

- Small-cap growth: 1937 at -49.32%

- Small-cap value: 1937 at -50.24%

The best decade:

- Small-cap growth: the 1950s, at 17.6% a year

- Small-cap value: the 1980s, at 21.6% a year

The worst decade:

- Small-cap growth: the 2000s at -1.4% a year

- Small-cap value: the 1930s, at 1.8% a year[30]

---

29   Arithmetic annualized return.

30   Ibbotson, *2020 SBBI Yearbook*, 2.12-2.19, 8.4-8.7.

After analyzing the data for our 90-year test period, I find that putting 20% of the total equities in small companies gives us an excellent mix. Notice that we've maintained the 50:50 split between growth and value stocks within each category of large and small companies.

Our portfolio is starting to look genuinely diversified, with a really nice mix of different kinds of investments. Take a look:

STEP FIVE
DIVERSIFY WITH SMALL COMPANIES

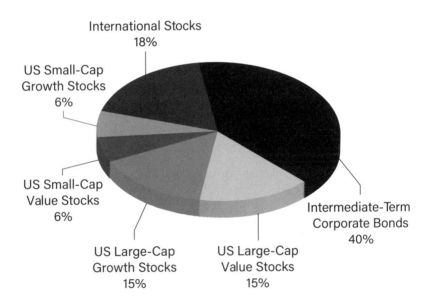

Put it to the test.

Here's how the portfolio performed:

THE PERFECT FINANCIAL STORM TEST: STEP FIVE ($100,000 initial portfolio with a 5.5% inflation-protected annual distribution, tested against every 40-year time frame since 1930)			
WILL YOUR MONEY LAST 40 YEARS?			
	Success Rate	Shortest Time to Depletion in 100% of Cases Tested*	Shortest Time to Depletion in 96% of Cases Tested**
Step One: Intermediate-term corporate bonds	2%	14 years	14 years
Step Two: US stocks, large companies	45%	17 years	18 years
Step Three: International stocks	37%	19 years	19 years
Step Four: US stocks, growth & value	53%	20 years	22 years
Step Five: US stocks, large and small	67%	21 years	24 years
*Includes every 40-year time frame since 1930. **Does not include 40-year time frames starting in 1937 and 1969.			

When we diversify with stocks from large and small companies, our shortest time to depletion is still a long way from our goal of 40 years. But the percentage of time frames that did make it to 40 years has improved nicely, up to 67%. We're ⅔ of the way to a 100% success rate.

Step Six: Eliminate Dead Wood

In this step, we will evaluate each and every investment area to see if there are any that don't pull their weight. In other words, can we improve on the portfolio by dropping one or more areas? As you might expect (why else would we include this step?), there is an asset class we can drop to generate an improvement in the performance of the portfolio.

That area is small-cap growth. Small-company growth stocks decrease the return of the portfolio and increase its risk. Heh, that's not a good combination. (There are times when small-cap growth stocks knock the lights out, but not enough to help the portfolio across all 51 of our 40-year time frames.) So we will replace small-cap growth with small-cap value to maintain the proper proportion in small-cap stocks, which is now 12% of the total portfolio.

Here's how it looks so far:

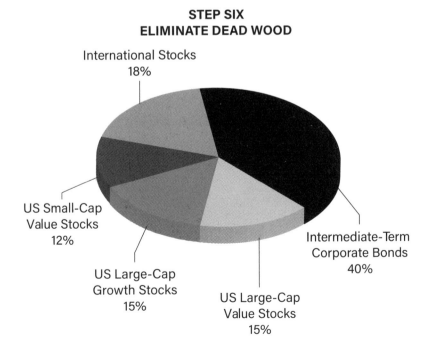

STEP SIX
ELIMINATE DEAD WOOD

International Stocks
18%

US Small-Cap
Value Stocks
12%

US Large-Cap
Growth Stocks
15%

US Large-Cap
Value Stocks
15%

Intermediate-Term
Corporate Bonds
40%

Put it to the test.

We continue to improve our portfolio, by all metrics, but especially our most important one: how long it will last. Here are the numbers:

THE PERFECT FINANCIAL STORM TEST: STEP SIX ($100,000 initial portfolio with a 5.5% inflation-protected annual distribution, tested against every 40-year time frame since 1930)			
WILL YOUR MONEY LAST 40 YEARS?			
	Success Rate	Shortest Time to Depletion in 100% of cases tested*	Shortest Time to Depletion in 96% of cases tested**
Step One: Intermediate-term corporate bonds	2%	14 years	14 years
Step Two: US stocks, large companies	45%	17 years	18 years
Step Three: International stocks	37%	19 years	19 years
Step Four: US stocks, growth & value	53%	20 years	22 years
Step Five: US stocks, large and small	67%	21 years	24 years
Step Six: Eliminate dead wood	78%	22 years	29 years
*Includes every 40-year time frame since 1930. **Does not include 40-year time frames starting in 1937 and 1969.			

In this step we see the clearest evidence so far of how devastating it can be to begin your retirement in a year that sees a dramatic downturn in the markets, as we did in 1937 and 1969. In the time frame starting in 1937, the portfolio we've built so far ran out of money in just 22 years; starting in 1969, it ran out in 24 years. But when we eliminate those time frames, our portfolio lasts at least 29 years.

And with that 78% success rate, we're getting much closer to our goal.

Step Seven: Apply Value Tilt

As we saw in Step Four, growth and value stocks tend to perform better in different financial climates. Either one can do well in a given market, but it's unusual for both to do well at the same time. That's why it helps our portfolio to invest in both. But while growth stocks are exciting to own (remember our example of a young Microsoft or Google), value stocks are like slow-moving steamers that provide the diversification with growth to build the equity foundation for our All-Weather Retirement Portfolio.

We can take advantage of that long-term growth by applying something called a "value tilt"—we take some money out of growth stocks so we have more to invest in value stocks. By tilting the large-cap US equities 2 to 1 in favor of value versus growth, we optimize our blend. In other words, we put twice as much money in large-cap value stocks as we have in large-cap growth.

It's worth noting here that by tilting in favor of value stocks, you give up bigger returns when growth-oriented stocks are in favor, like they were in the 1990s. However, the assurance of having a portfolio that will outlive you is well worth giving up the *possibility* of that particular market gain.

> The assurance of having a portfolio that will outlive you is well worth giving up the *possibility* of that particular market gain.

Here's how the portfolio looks now:

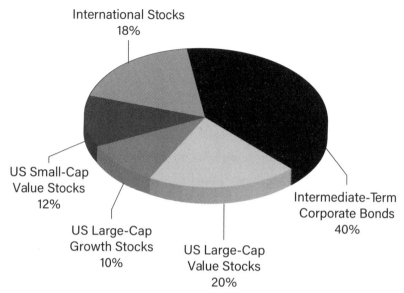

STEP SEVEN
APPLY VALUE TILT

International Stocks
18%

US Small-Cap
Value Stocks
12%

US Large-Cap
Growth Stocks
10%

US Large-Cap
Value Stocks
20%

Intermediate-Term
Corporate Bonds
40%

Put it to the test.

Let's see if the addition of stocks gets us closer to our ultimate goal of providing an inflation-protected income of 5.5% per year for 40 years.

THE PERFECT FINANCIAL STORM TEST: STEP SEVEN
($100,000 initial portfolio with a 5.5% inflation-protected annual distribution, tested against every 40-year time frame since 1930)

WILL YOUR MONEY LAST 40 YEARS?

	Success Rate	Shortest Time to Depletion in 100% of Cases Tested*	Shortest Time to Depletion in 96% of Cases Tested**
Step One: Intermediate-term corporate bonds	2%	14 years	14 years
Step Two: US stocks, large companies	45%	17 years	18 years
Step Three: International stocks	37%	19 years	19 years
Step Four: US stocks, growth & value	53%	20 years	22 years
Step Five: US stocks, large and small	67%	21 years	24 years
Step Six: Eliminate dead wood	78%	22 years	29 years
Step Seven: Apply value tilt	84%	23 years	33 years

*Includes every 40-year time frame since 1930.
**Does not include 40-year time frames starting in 1937 and 1969.

Our analysis in this step makes a strong case for the power of applying that value tilt in this step. All the numbers improved substantially.

Step Eight: Adjust the Ratio of Stocks and Bonds

We started out with a blend of 60% stocks and 40% bonds. We did this because many retirement books suggest this, and it's a standard recommendation among advisors. But I wanted to see how that mix compares to other ratios. Would adjusting the blend get us a better outcome?

I looked at a blend of 80% stocks and 20% bonds, as well as 70% stocks and 30% bonds. I ran our current portfolio through the PFS Test with those two blends, as well as the standard 60/40 blend. In each case, I allocated the money I took from bonds proportionately across the different types of equities. When all was said and done (and my calculator was asking for paid medical leave), I found that the 70/30 mix was the "sweet spot" in terms of producing the best success rates and extending the amount of time it took for the portfolio to be depleted.

Here's what our portfolio looks like:

STEP EIGHT
ADJUST THE RATIO OF STOCKS & BONDS

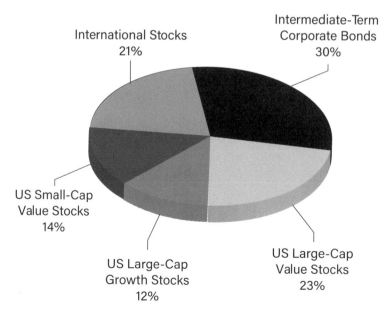

International Stocks
21%

Intermediate-Term
Corporate Bonds
30%

US Small-Cap
Value Stocks
14%

US Large-Cap
Growth Stocks
12%

US Large-Cap
Value Stocks
23%

Put it to the test.

When we apply the Perfect Financial Storm Test, it's clear this adjustment improves our portfolio substantially. Take a look.

THE PERFECT FINANCIAL STORM TEST: STEP EIGHT ($100,000 initial portfolio with a 5.5% inflation-protected annual distribution, tested against every 40-year time frame since 1930)			
WILL YOUR MONEY LAST 40 YEARS?			
	Success Rate	Shortest Time to Depletion in 100% of Cases Tested*	Shortest Time to Depletion in 96% of Cases Tested**
Step One: Intermediate-term corporate bonds	2.0%	14 years	14 years
Step Two: US stocks, large companies	45%	17 years	18 years
Step Three: International stocks	37%	19 years	19 years
Step Four: US stocks, growth & value	53%	20 years	22 years
Step Five: US stocks, large and small	67%	21 years	24 years
Step Six: Eliminate dead wood	78%	22 years	29 years
Step Seven: Apply value tilt	84%	23 years	33 years
Step Eight: Adjust ratio of stocks & bonds	94%	24 years	37 years
*Includes every 40-year time frame since 1930. **Does not include 40-year time frames starting in 1937 and 1969.			

Adjusting our ratio of stocks to bonds from 60/40 to 70/30 improved our portfolio's performance in every category. With a 70/30 blend of equities to bonds, the portfolio would have lasted 40 years in 94% of our time frames. And in 96% of cases it lasted 37 years. Clearly we're closing in on our goal of a 100% success rate at having our portfolio last the full 40 years. In spite of the fact that so many other books—and so many financial advisors—recommend a 60/40 ratio of stocks to bonds, the data you see here clearly demonstrate that the 70/30 ratio in fact gives you a more stable portfolio. We're now within spittin' distance of our goal, with a portfolio that lasts 40 years 94% of the time.

We have two more steps to get all the way there.

Step Nine: Optimize International Stocks with Emerging Markets

Step Nine is a bit challenging. This time we're going to take some money from our international stocks, which up to now have been exclusively from developed countries, and put it into international emerging markets. "Emerging markets" refers to countries that are not yet considered developed countries. Examples include:

- Brazil
- South Africa
- Mexico
- Chile
- Fiji
- Peru
- Russia

As an asset class, emerging markets is a volatile category, but it generally has a high rate of return over time. The nice thing about it is that it tends to move differently from everything else in the portfolio. So when the US large companies are not doing well, emerging markets are often going great. That's want you want in a diversified portfolio: dissimilar movements in different asset classes.

After extensive testing I found that the optimum balance is to allocate about 30% of your total international market stocks to emerging markets. Since international stocks make up 21% of your total portfolio, we'll keep 15% of the total portfolio in stocks from international developed countries, and place 6% of the total portfolio in stocks from emerging markets. Our total investment in international markets hasn't changed—it's still at 21% of the total portfolio. We're just dividing it between two classes of international stocks.

Here's what our portfolio looks like now:

STEP NINE
OPTIMIZE INTERNATIONAL STOCKS
WITH EMERGING MARKETS

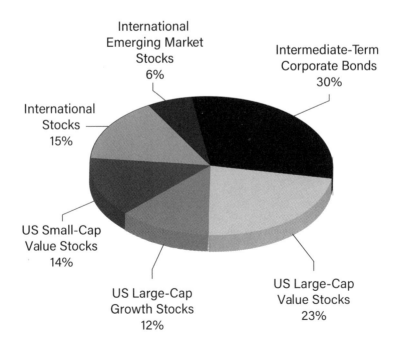

International Emerging Market Stocks 6%

Intermediate-Term Corporate Bonds 30%

International Stocks 15%

US Small-Cap Value Stocks 14%

US Large-Cap Growth Stocks 12%

US Large-Cap Value Stocks 23%

Put it to the test.

THE PERFECT FINANCIAL STORM TEST: STEP NINE ($100,000 initial portfolio with a 5.5% inflation-protected annual distribution, tested against every 40-year time frame since 1930)			
WILL YOUR MONEY LAST 40 YEARS?			
	Success Rate	Shortest Time to Depletion in 100% of Cases Tested*	Shortest Time to Depletion in 96% of Cases Tested**
Step One: Intermediate-term corporate bonds	2%	14 years	14 years
Step Two: US stocks, large companies	45%	17 years	18 years
Step Three: International stocks	37%	19 years	19 years
Step Four: US stocks, growth & value	53%	20 years	22 years
Step Five: US stocks, large and small	67%	21 years	24 years
Step Six: Eliminate dead wood	78%	22 years	29 years
Step Seven: Apply value tilt	84%	23 years	33 years
Step Eight: Adjust ratio of stocks & bonds	94%	24 years	37 years
Step Nine: Emerging market stocks	96%	24 years	40 years
*Includes every 40-year time frame since 1930. **Does not include 40-year time frames starting in 1937 and 1969.			

This is where things get really exciting. With the addition of stocks from emerging markets, our portfolio is now well enough diversified to last 40 years—most of the time. It was only in those two horrendous time frames that it didn't survive. A 96% success rate is pretty darn good. But we don't want to bet your retirement on the chance that you won't fall into that 4% that didn't make it.

That's why we have one more step. We'll get there … you'll see.

Step Ten: Apply the 8-Year Rule

At this point the results of our Perfect Financial Storm Test are looking pretty terrific. By the end of Step Nine, our All-Weather Retirement Portfolio boasted a success rate of a solid 96%. Yep, our portfolio lasted the full 40 years in more than 96% of the 40-year time frames we tested. That's pretty impressive, especially when you consider we were taking a 5.5% inflation-protected initial distribution. Your average run-of-the-mill portfolio would be hard pressed to make that claim, let alone actually pass the Perfect Financial Storm Test.

But what about the other 4%? You know how I am—I'm all in when it comes to creating a portfolio you can feel confident will provide you with income for as long as you need it, no matter what kind of stormy weather the market has in store for you. In my book, 96% still isn't good enough. But what's keeping us from hitting that 100% mark?

It's all about those pesky perfect financial storm scenarios, when the market takes a terrible hit during the earliest years of your retirement. In our 90-year test period, that's what happened in 1937 and 1969. If you'd retired in those years, you'd have had a really tough time recovering enough to keep that 5.5% income stream going for the full 40 years, even with our fully diversified portfolio. As we see in the table on page

124, when we include those years in our PFS Test, if you'd retired in 1937 your money would have run out in as little as 24 years. If you were 60 years old when you started drawing that retirement income, at 84 you'd have been broke and asking, "Do you want fries with that?" at your local fast-food place. If you'd had your retirement party in 1969, your portfolio would have lasted 29 years—not much better. You'd have been flat out of cash by the time you turned 89.

But is there one more step we can apply to create a portfolio that would have weathered even those brutal storms? Can we create a financial storm shelter to protect you even when a twice-in-90-year disaster strikes?

Funny you should ask.

The answer is yes. Of course there is.[31]

That perfect financial storm shelter is a little something I call the 8-Year Rule. It's so called because you only apply it if the worst of the worst financial storms hits in those sensitive years when your retirement portfolio is most vulnerable—the first 8 years after you retire. After that you're on autopilot. Here's how it works:

1. During the first 8 years after you retire, at the end of each 12-month period you'll check your year-end balance before you take any disbursement in the following year. If that year-end (end of the 12-month cycle) balance is less than 75% of what it was when you started your retirement—that is, when you began taking distributions—do not take your annual inflation increase for the coming year. For instance, if you retire on July 1, on the following June 30—and every June 30 for the first 8 years—you'll check your balance. If

---

31   As I am required to mention, even though this approach is successful in every 40-year time frame since 1930, there can be no assurance it will work going forward, because it's possible there will be a financial storm even worse than anything we've seen in the past 90 years.

it's less than 75% of what it was when you retired, apply the 8-Year Rule. For the rest of the year, don't worry about it. Even if the market hits some turbulence, you're good.

2. Continue to skip adding the inflation adjustment to your disbursement until your year-end assessment indicates account balance is at least 90% of the amount you started with. When it reaches that 90% mark, resume adjusting your disbursement by the previous year's inflation rate.

3. When your portfolio grows to more than 110% of what it was when you retired, you can "catch up" to what you would be receiving if you hadn't applied the rule. Simply take the income you drew in the last year in which you took an inflation adjustment, multiply that amount by 1 plus the inflation rate for the first year you applied the 8-Year Rule and didn't bump up your income, then repeat the calculation for each year up to the current year. That will tell you what your income would be if you'd been adjusting for inflation all along. Bump your income up to that amount and go on with life, and be happy.

That's it. That's all you need to do.

Put it to the test.

Remember, we haven't changed the portfolio at all in this step. All we did was apply the 8-Year Rule, which tells us to skip adjusting our income for inflation, if—*and only if*—our account balance at the end of the retirement year was less than 75% of what it was when we first started taking income. And we only did that during the first 8 years of retirement. Pretty painless.

Let's see how it pencils out.

THE PERFECT FINANCIAL STORM TEST: STEP TEN
($100,000 initial portfolio with a 5.5% inflation-protected annual distribution, tested against every 40-year time frame since 1930)

WILL YOUR MONEY LAST 40 YEARS?

	Success Rate	Shortest Time to Depletion in 100% of Cases Tested*	Shortest Time to Depletion in 96% of Cases Tested**
Step One: Intermediate-term corporate bonds	2%	14 years	14 years
Step Two: US stocks, large companies	45%	17 years	18 years
Step Three: International stocks	37%	19 years	19 years
Step Four: US stocks, growth & value	53%	20 years	22 years
Step Five: US stocks, large and small	67%	21 years	24 years
Step Six: Eliminate dead wood	78%	22 years	29 years
Step Seven: Apply value tilt	84%	23 years	33 years
Step Eight: Adjust ratio of stocks & bonds	94%	24 years	37 years
Step Nine: Emerging market stocks	96%	24 years	40 years
Step Ten: The 8-Year Rule	100%	40 years	40 years

*Includes every 40-year time frame since 1930.
**Does not include 40-year time frames starting in 1937 and 1969.

As you can see, when we add the 8-Year Rule to our All-Weather Retirement Portfolio and run it through our Perfect Financial Storm

Test, something wonderful happens. (*Drum roll ...*) Our portfolio lasts 40 years, 100% of the time—even when we include the 40-year time frames starting in 1937 and 1969, the worst years the market experienced in our entire 90-year test period.

Let me say it again: *The All-Weather Retirement Portfolio lasts 40 years, with an inflation-protected 5.5% initial annual income, in 100% of the 40-year time frames from 1930 to 2019.*

I've taken you through the ten steps you can take to build a portfolio that will provide you with a worry-free, spendable cash flow for the rest of your life.

This portfolio:

- took on the worst the financial markets had to offer since 1930,

- provided you with an initial annual, inflation-protected distribution rate of 5.5%,

- *and still had money left at the end of a 40-year time frame!*

Hopefully, your retirement years won't take you through financial storms as severe as the worst-case scenarios we used here in our Perfect Financial Storm Test. But as the results of the test show, if you do encounter a similar disaster you'll still be able to relax and enjoy your worry-free retirement. That's what the All-Weather Retirement Portfolio will do for you.

The All-Weather Retirement Portfolio

To summarize, we started with a portfolio made up exclusively of intermediate-term corporate bonds. We looked at every 40-year rolling time frame since 1930 and found that our bond portfolio lasted the full 40 years in only 2% of those time frames. We then went through eight more steps to improve our portfolio by diversifying our investments across a variety of asset classes, and saw improvements with each step. With the addition of our 8-Year Rule in the final step, we found our way to an income-for-life portfolio that provided a 5.5% inflation-protected income for 40 years 100% of the time.

The result is our basic, worry-free, All-Weather Retirement Portfolio. It looks like this:

- 30% intermediate-term corporate bonds

- 49% US stocks

- 23% large-cap value

- 12% large-cap growth

- 14% small-cap value

- 21% international stocks

- 15% developed countries

- 6% emerging markets

Now, how do you find the right stocks and bonds to buy for each segment of your portfolio? And what if your growth stocks take off, and you discover they've increased in value so they account for 20% of your portfolio? What will you do?

Never fear. In the coming chapters we'll explore the best way to buy blocks of stocks to make up each of the asset classes in your portfolio, and then learn how to maintain it so it continues to perform as it should throughout your retirement years.

Chapter Ten

Rebalancing Your Portfolio

O nce you've done your homework, diversified your assets, and created an All-Weather Retirement Portfolio that can withstand the perfect financial storm, you'll need to keep an eye on your progress and make the necessary adjustments to keep it on course. You've invested your money in a financial market that, like the weather, can change rapidly. Don't be caught unprepared. Remember, too, that with asset allocation as your fundamental strategy, you've designed your portfolio to include investments that move in different directions in any given economic climate. It follows, then, that as you sail through time, some of your assets will quickly increase in value, others will grow more slowly, and some will even decline. As a result, your portfolio will no longer reflect the percentages we decided on in Chapter Nine—you'll have too much of your money in one asset class and not enough in another. You'll be out of balance. What's an investor to do?

The solution is to *rebalance* your portfolio. That means you'll sell a portion of your assets in some categories, and buy more in other categories, to restore that balance of return versus risk, with the optimum percentage of assets in each asset class.

Keep in mind that our goal is not to design a portfolio that *just* gets you the highest return on your investments. We're not trying to hit home runs here. We want you to be able to expect *a reasonable return* while *minimizing your risk,* and we do that through proper diversification—not just when we create your portfolio, but on an ongoing basis throughout your retirement years. The only way to maintain that particular approach to diversification is through rebalancing.

> We want you to be able to expect a reasonable return while minimizing your risk.

It's probably no surprise to find that investment advisors differ in their views about the best way to rebalance your portfolio. How often should you do it? How far out of balance should you be before you move money? And if one of your investments is way out of balance because it's been making money hand over fist, do you really want to sell some of it just to keep your allocation percentages in balance?

At first glance the answers may seem to be lost in a thick fog. Not to worry. At the risk of pushing this metaphor too far out to sea, I'm about to light a beacon that will show you how to guide your ship safely into port.

Four Ways to Rebalance Your Portfolio

There are four rebalancing techniques that are favorites among advisors and investors. Some are tried-and-true methods the pros rely on year after year. Others will probably make you feel good in the moment, but they can put you in jeopardy when the next perfect financial storm rolls in. Our task here is to find the approach that will best serve our goal of providing you with a worry-free income for *all* of your retirement years.

Let's take a look at the most popular rebalancing techniques:

1. Put more money on the winner

2. The Robin Hood method

3. The calendar method

4. The trigger method

Put more money on the winner

If an investment area has done well, your first response is likely to be to put more money into it, right? Out of all the rebalancing methods, "put more money on the winner" is emotionally the easiest to do. You feel good about putting more money into the fund that has gone up, fully expecting you'll see even larger returns when the value of the fund continues to increase.

However, we are not after what feels good; we're after results. And while you'll feel good *and* see good results as long as that one asset class continues to do well, what happens when the economic tide turns and the asset takes a tumble? If you've allowed your portfolio to become wildly unbalanced in favor of that asset, you'll have lost the protection of diversification—and you'll be in big trouble.

As difficult as it may be to resist the temptation to put more money on the winning portion of your portfolio—*don't do it!*

The Robin Hood method

The Robin Hood method is in essence the opposite of "put money on the winner." It takes money from the best-performing area and gives it to the worst area on a monthly or quarterly basis. (All the other areas are left alone.) This is counterintuitive, and contrary to everything your heart wants you to do. You want to put more money on the winner. Why on earth would you want to put more money into something that is going down?

First, because that's the only way to maintain the proportions among different asset classes that we established in Chapter Nine. But more importantly, remember why we established those proportions—and the diversification they represent—in the first place. It's because eventually, what goes up … you know the drill. Also, what goes down must eventually go back up. That's why we have all those different elements in your portfolio, so that when one asset class goes down, another will be on the rise. That's your protection against the perfect financial storm.

The Robin Hood method is a big step in the right direction, because it applies the key principle of maintaining a well-balanced portfolio. But we can refine that approach and get an even better result. Read on.

The calendar method

With the calendar method you simply rebalance at regular, pre-determined time intervals. That can mean rebalancing daily (a real pain), weekly (still painful), monthly, quarterly, semi-annually, or annually. If any asset class deviates from your target percentage by any amount—even if it's as little as 0.1%—you move money around to bring each investment class back to its original percentage of the total portfolio.

Most advocates of the calendar method rebalance monthly, quarterly, semi-annually, or annually. Again applying the Perfect Financial Storm Test, our research demonstrates that rebalancing quarterly is the clear winner. Not only does that give you the best return, it also has the least amount of risk. That's precisely the result we're after.

The trigger method

While the Robin Hood method looks only at the best- and worst-performing investment areas, with the trigger method we look at *each investment area* every day, and evaluate *how much* it varies from our original allocation. (If you need to, refer back to page 130 in Chapter Nine, "Ten Steps to a Worry-Free Income for Life," to review the percentages we assigned to each asset class in your portfolio.) If any area is off *by a certain percentage*, then it triggers rebalancing. If it isn't, then we leave it alone.

Advisors differ on the percentage amount that will trigger a rebalance (once again, no surprise here), but most take action when the allocation is off somewhere between 2.0% and 10%. I've run the numbers through our Perfect Financial Storm Test, using the 40-year period from 1973 through 2012. The results indicate that rebalancing when an asset class is off by 2% to 5% offers the best return with the least amount of risk. The percentage you apply depends on whether the asset is in a taxable portfolio or not.

If your investment is in a taxable portfolio, any time you sell an asset you're subject to taxation on any gains, which is precisely what happens when you rebalance. In that scenario the higher trigger of 5% makes sense, so you maintain your asset allocation without paying more in taxes than you need to. For the investments you hold in a nontaxable account, such as an IRA, you use 2% as your trigger. That way, with no worry about additional tax liability you'll be able to reduce your risk significantly, because your portfolio will deviate less from the original allocation we arrived at in Chapter Nine.

All of this is useful information. Make a mental note of it while we look at the next approach to rebalancing.

The best of the best: The calendar and trigger methods combined

Of our four favorite approaches to rebalancing, three serve us well: the Robin Hood, trigger, and calendar methods. Of those, we can eliminate the Robin Hood method because it only addresses the best- and worst-performing areas of your portfolio and ignores the others. The calendar and trigger methods rebalance all segments of the portfolio, so they in effect make Robin Hood irrelevant.

Now let's take it one step further. What if we combine the calendar and the trigger methods to create a rebalancing method that's truly outstanding?

Here's how it works:

- Calendar method: Rebalance your portfolio quarterly.

- Trigger method: Rebalance any assets that deviate from our target percentage of the total portfolio by more than 5% of your entire portfolio if it's in a taxable account, or 2% if in a non-taxable account, like an IRA.

Let's look at an example. We've established your target for the emerging markets segment of your portfolio as 6%. In your taxable portfolio we would rebalance if it grows to 11% (5% more than the target), or 8% if it's in an IRA (2% more than the target). We'd also rebalance if that segment falls to 1% in a taxable account or 4% in an IRA.

Combining the calendar and trigger methods delivers the best of both worlds. That is, on a quarterly basis, apply the trigger method and see if you need to rebalance. If rebalancing is triggered, do so. If not, relax until the next quarter comes around.

How much does rebalancing help? A recent study found that rebalancing, as part of a disciplined approach to investing, increased the return on investment by an average of 0.89% per year.[32] As you can imagine, when that additional annual return compounds year after year, the benefit to your portfolio will be substantial. Very few strategies give you that kind of benefit without an added cost. (This assumes, of course, that you incur no transaction fees when you move money from one to another, and especially no new sales loads, which are much higher—a key reason to choose no-load funds.)

Putting It All to Work

It's easy to see how critical it is to rebalance your portfolio on a consistent basis. It's the only way to maintain the highly effective asset allocation we established through our "Ten Steps to a Worry-Free Income for Life" in Chapter Nine. But as important as it is, study after study shows that most individuals, if left to rebalance the portfolio themselves, simply don't do it. They get busy, they allow emotions to govern their decisions, they can't bring themselves to sell the investment area that did really well that quarter, or they succumb to any number of other reasons to deviate from our well-researched plan. You can't afford to do that.

That's why I recommend you avoid all those pitfalls by automating the process. If you're managing your portfolio yourself, ask if

---

32   Kieran Osborne, "What Are the Benefits of Portfolio Rebalancing?" *Mission Wealth*, May 12, 2020, https://missionwealth.com/what-are-the-benefits-of-portfolio-rebalancing/.

the company that holds your money (generally called the custodian) can do it for you. If you have an investment advisor, have him take responsibility for it. That way the process will be handled for you on a systemized, disciplined, emotionless basis. Most advisors can and will do this as part of the service they provide. I'll explain how you can find a great one in Chapter Twelve.

Chapter Eleven

The Best Way to (Mutual) Fund Your All-Weather Retirement Portfolio

Now that you know *what kinds* of stocks and bonds to invest in, how will you decide which ones you'll actually buy? With literally thousands to choose from within each of the asset classes we discussed in Chapter Nine, deciding which ones to include in your portfolio may seem like a daunting task. What if you find a great-looking small-cap value stock, but the company goes belly up in a year?

Rest assured, there is a solution: Mutual funds.

With a single share in a mutual fund, you actually buy into hundreds of stocks (or more) selected by the mutual fund manager. Not only do you get the benefit of his or her expertise in choosing promising stocks or bonds, you also minimize your business risk (the risk that a business might fail) by spreading your dollars across many different companies. That means that if a single stock doesn't perform as well as the manager expects, or, worse, if the company goes

139

bankrupt, the loss will be barely a blip on the screen when it's just one of three hundred or more stocks in your mutual fund.

Mutual funds also offer you the opportunity to buy a large number of stocks or bonds within a particular asset class. For example, some funds are made up of small-cap value stocks, while others buy large-cap growth stocks. By applying the principles we discussed in Chapter Nine, and allocating the appropriate percentage of your nest egg to mutual funds specializing in each of our chosen asset classes, you can create that All-Weather Retirement Portfolio that will provide you with a worry-free income for life.

Choosing the Right Mutual Fund

Granted, you still have some decisions to make. Opting to invest in mutual funds doesn't mean you can retire your thinking cap. There are more than 20,000 mutual funds, some with sales charges and some without. Some are brand new and others have a track record. Some work well in a portfolio and others don't. There are so many mutual fund variables and so many options ... what's the average person to do?

Fortunately, there are people and organizations that track these things. The Morningstar financial services company is one of the best. The company tracks more than 20,000 funds, including the newest ones as they emerge. All that research is available on the Morningstar website, www.morningstar.com. Still, the sheer volume of information means you'll have homework to do to make sure you find the funds that best suit your needs. The Morningstar website has a vast array of tools to help you find the information that's most relevant to you.

Before you dive into all that research, let's walk through some key issues that will help you make sound choices. Then, in case you're still not ready to make the leap on your own, I'll share my current personal favorites with you.

First, let's take a look at 11 key factors that determine whether a given fund will help—or hurt—your portfolio. Here they are, in order of their priority:

1. Your investment philosophy

2. The asset class the mutual fund invests in

3. Style drift

4. The expense ratio

5. Loads, transaction costs, and other fees

6. The fund manager

7. Tax efficiency

8. Conflict of interest

9. Ease of rebalancing

10. Reporting and statements

11. The fund's ranking within its peer group

Your investment philosophy

In Chapter Eight, "The Two Most Important Questions," we considered the two questions that determine your personal investment philosophy. Based on whether or not you believe you can time the market—that is, predict the next rising or falling trend—or pick the next hot stock, you fall into one of several categories of investors, and choose your mutual funds accordingly.

If you're looking for the next hot stock, mutual funds may not be for you. You'll have to spend your time analyzing individual companies and trying to beat the pros in spotting the next Google. I wish you luck—you'll need it.

Or, if you believe you can predict which market sector will lead the next upward or downward trend, you can find mutual funds that specialize in, say, tech stocks or energy stocks. But beware. Surely you've heard how many market wizards lost gazillions of dollars when the dot-com bubble burst. They never saw that coming. Did you? What if you had bet your retirement on it? No, it's not a pretty picture.

Fortunately, as we've discovered in the last few chapters, you don't need to rely on luck or a crystal ball. After looking at the research and factoring in my own experience, we decided that the soundest investment philosophy is one based on asset allocation, particularly when you're investing for retirement income. Asset allocation, or diversification, suggests you diversify your investments to get the best expected return for a given level of risk. To get that optimum balance between return and risk, you blend investments from several different asset classes that move in different directions—that is, some gain and some lose—in any given economic climate. You can do that by buying several different mutual funds that specialize in one or another of those asset classes.

The asset class the mutual fund invests in

If your investment philosophy is the diversified, asset allocation approach, then you need funds that invest solely in stocks or bonds of a given type. There are funds designed specifically for this purpose. They're called "asset class funds," and they're usually named according to the asset class they invest in. For example, you can buy a Vanguard Large-Cap Growth Fund, a Dimensional Fund Advisors (DFA) Small-Cap Value Fund, and so forth.

You can also find excellent funds that are currently invested in a specific asset class, even though they're not defined by that criterion, so they may not technically be "asset class funds." These funds need to be monitored closely on an ongoing basis for what we call "style drift" (see the following section), but they're well worth considering.

To design your portfolio to pass the Perfect Financial Storm Test, as in Chapter Nine, you'll need one or more each of:

- Intermediate-term corporate bond fund

- US large-cap value fund

- US large-cap growth fund

- US small-cap value fund

- International fund

- International emerging market fund

Style drift

Once you've selected a fund (or funds) in each asset category, you want it to *stay in that category*. In other words, you don't want to see signs of style drift. If you're trying to build your portfolio around investments with dissimilar movements, you've got to be able to count on each fund to stay within its style. For example, if your value fund changes to a growth fund, then you've lost your diversification—so your worry-free portfolio, and hence your income, is in jeopardy.

When your goal is a worry-free income for life, style drift can be devastating. A drift from *any* asset class to another can cause the portfolio to suffer, and you could be out of money when you've still got cruise tickets to buy.

You can decrease the chances of running into style drift by buying designated asset class funds. However, you'll still need to monitor them for style drift on an ongoing basis. It's just too critical a threat to the durability of your portfolio to assume you're immune. You can monitor them at the Morningstar website, www.morningstar.com, and it's much easier than you might expect. In fact, when you look at your fund's page on Morningstar, you'll see a grid called the "Morningstar Style Box," which shows you the asset class style of your fund. (If you need help using the box, you can click on a tiny "?" that will open a tutorial of sorts.)

Be sure to check your funds from time to time, or you can sign up for a premium Morningstar subscription and have them send you emails with news of anything going on with your funds.

The expense ratio

The expense ratio is the amount of money the investment company charges you every year to administer the fund. It's calculated as a percentage of the amount of money you have invested. A percentage is essentially a ratio (25% is the same as 25:100), hence the term "expense ratio."

Administrative expenses are a necessary cost of doing business (like any other enterprise, it costs money to manage investments), so there's an expense ratio associated with every mutual fund. Be aware, though, that there are firms that take these fees to an extreme. In 2007, a search for the fund with the highest expense ratio found one that came in at a whopping 18.7%.[33] You read that right: 18.7% of your investment would have gone straight to pay the company's administrative costs. As of this writing, one of the costliest funds out there is charging 11.8%. Clearly it's a factor you need to check before you buy into a fund.

It may seem obvious that as a general rule, the lower the expense ratio the better. But there are exceptions. For example, a fund with a

---

33   Amanda Kish, "The World's Most Expensive Mutual Fund," *The Motley Fool*, November 15, 2016, https://www.fool.com/investing/mutual-funds/2007/05/29/the-worlds-most-expensive-mutual-fund.aspx.

bargain basement expense ratio is no bargain if the fund's performance is poor, if it carries too much risk, or if it suffers a bad case of style drift. Consider this factor as just one of the points you'll need to evaluate, and compare expense ratios along with other factors among funds of the same asset class. For example, you'll want to compare a US small-cap value fund with another US small-cap value fund. It isn't appropriate to compare a US stock fund to an international fund, since international funds will naturally have higher expenses.

Loads, transaction costs, and ... marketing fees?

Some mutual funds carry fees over and above the necessary administrative fees, but you can avoid paying them simply by choosing funds that don't charge them. I encourage you to do that. The most common types of fees to look out for are front- or back-end loads, transaction fees, and 12b-1 fees.

Loads. In mutual fund lingo, "load" is just another word for "sales charge." Some funds charge you up front just for the privilege of putting your hard-earned dollars into them. Others use a back-end charge, so they lock you in for a number of years even if you're unhappy and want to get out. Either way, a load is just an additional cost—on top of the expense ratio—that comes straight out of your pocket, then most of it goes into the pocket of the broker as a commission for recommending the fund.

Like the expense ratio, a load is assessed as a percentage of the amount of your investment, however it's not an annual cost—you only pay when you buy or sell the fund. The problem with a sales load is that the percentages tend to be much higher than those of an expense ratio, and it's money that comes straight out of your investment. For example, if you invest $100,000 in a fund with a 5% front-end load, only $95,000 will actually be deposited in the fund to go to work for you.

Keep in mind that the sales load is applied each time you buy a fund (in the case of a front-end load) or sell it (if it has a back-end load). That means that each time you rebalance your portfolio you'll have to pay that fee for any asset class you hold in a loaded fund.[34] Those costs take a serious bite out of your returns.

In my humble opinion (okay, maybe not so humble) you should only use no-load funds—those with no front- or back-end load. Research indicates that load funds *do not* perform better than no-load funds, so why spend money you don't need to spend?

Transaction costs. Many of the funds that don't have sales loads charge transaction fees instead. A key difference here is that transaction fees are applied when you buy *and* sell the fund. On the bright side, these costs tend to be much lower than sales loads, and funds that have transaction costs often have particularly low expense ratios. Your transaction fee might be based on a percentage of your investment, but often it's a set cost per share, or in some cases it's a flat amount regardless of the amount of the investment or number of shares.

There are a number of different types of funds and various circumstances that carry transaction costs. For example, exchange-traded funds, more commonly referred to as ETFs,[35] generally have them, and some advisors charge them when moving no-load funds from one account to another. The key is to know they're out there, and find out whether they apply to the fund—or the transaction—you're considering. It's important because, again, if you're rebalancing quarterly (as you should be) and taking monthly distributions, these costs can really add up.

---

34   There is one exception here, and it applies to a loaded fund within a family of funds. See page 154 for details.

35   ETFs are funds that can be traded throughout the day, whereas most mutual fund transactions take place at the end of the day.

12b-1 fees. There are some mutual funds that carry a "hidden"[36] charge called a "12b-1 fee," so you can help pay for the marketing and advertising of the fund. I'm not kidding. This charge can be as much as 1% of the money you have invested—and you pay it *every year*.

I really don't like these funds, especially when they're charging the full additional 1% every year. With perhaps a sole exception for the American Family of Funds (see my explanation under "Loaded funds, if you have to," on page 154), there's no reason for you to take on that added expense.

The fund manager

When you find a fund that looks good, make sure there hasn't been a recent change in its manager. If so, you may want to set it aside and take another look a few years down the road. The strong performance in recent years might be due to one manager who did a great job, with no guarantee her replacement will do as well.

Want to know the truly scary part? The average age of a fund manager today is approximately 40 years old, with a tenure of around 4 years. You want someone who has seen and survived a down market. That means, if you're looking for a fund manager in 2021, he should have been in the business at least since the year 2008 and preferably since 2000. Before you settle on a fund, check the Morningstar website for information about the manager's history with the fund, experience, and past performance.

---

36   I say "hidden" because these fees are rarely disclosed in sales literature. You can find them if you're willing to do extra research on sites like Morningstar. They're also disclosed in the fund's prospectus, but have you ever tried to read one of those?

Tax efficiency

When your fund manager sells a stock or bond inside the mutual fund, and if that stock or bond has increased in value since he bought it, the increase in value, or "capital gain," is distributed to the mutual fund shareholders. This distribution is called a capital gain distribution and is taxable. Fund managers are required to distribute these capital gains once a year. If your investments are in an IRA or a retirement plan, you won't be liable for those taxes. If they're not, those taxes will take a big bite out of your money.

The more frequently the fund manager buys and sells stocks within the fund portfolio—also known as "turnover"—the greater the tax liability is likely to be. So when turnover is high, the fund's "tax efficiency" is poor. Less turnover means greater tax efficiency. That's what you want if the fund will be outside of your IRA or retirement plan.

Although tough to find, there are funds that specifically invest for non-IRA investments. These have lower turnover, and the managers apply other techniques to minimize tax ramifications. Often these funds state "low turnover" and other tax-efficient strategies in their prospectuses. Others put it out there, front and center, with the phrase "tax managed" or something similar in the name of the fund.

Conflict of interest

Beware of XYZ Brokerage Company selling XYZ funds. Sometimes representatives in these firms are offered incentives if they sell their own firm's funds. That can mean they have more motivation to increase their own bottom line than yours.

Ask if there are any conflicts of interest before you invest! Ask to see their Form ADV, which discloses any such conflicts. All investment advisors are required to file this document with the Securities and Exchange Commission (SEC) and make it available to investors.

Ease of rebalancing

Portfolios get out of balance, as we discussed in detail in Chapter Ten, "Rebalancing Your Portfolio," starting on page 131. But for now, just know that different asset classes grow at different rates—remember, that's precisely why you diversify. But when your international equities outpace your bonds, or your large-cap growth investments start to dwarf your large-cap value stocks, you'll need to rebalance—that is, sell some of one and buy more of the other—to maintain the percentages we decided on in Chapter Nine.

If you incur large fees each time you buy and sell portions of your funds, or if it takes days to move money from one fund to another (your money can't work for you while it's floating between fund A and fund B), you may lose more than you gain from rebalancing. You must have an easy way to put the portfolio back in balance *without* charges, and without missing days in the market. As you'll see later in this chapter, there are options out there that will make it easier—or more difficult— to rebalance. Either way, it should be on your list of things to consider.

Reporting and statements

Statements need to be easy to read. You would think that goes without saying, but it doesn't. For one fund I know, when you get your statement you actually have to multiply the fund value per share by the number of shares you own to find out how much you have. You'd think they could do that for you ...

Before you invest, ask to look at a statement. Is it simple to read? If not, can they explain it to you so it makes sense?

Ranking within peer group

How does the fund you're considering compare to others like it? How does your intermediate-term bond fund compare to other intermediate-term bond funds? How does that small-cap value fund stack up against other small-cap value funds? Has the fund been consistently in the upper half of its peer group? If not, why not?

> Statements need to be easy to read. You would think that goes without saying, but it doesn't.

You'll find answers to all these questions by using the filter system at the Morningstar website, which allows you to examine a multitude of factors. The sheer volume of information can seem a bit daunting, but be sure to at least consider risk, style drift, changes in management, and costs. You can also look at what kind of return a fund has generated over the past 3-, 5-, and 10-year periods, and compare that to others in its asset class. Be sure the time period you're looking at includes one or more years in which the economic climate in general was poor. Some funds do very well in good years, but perform terribly when times are tough.

Beware of a fund that made the top ten list in its category for a single year. Many times a fund will make the list because the manager took big risks the others in the category didn't take. He got lucky this year, but that could change next year. Choose consistency over hot and cold. If you find a fund that has been *consistently* in the top ten, or close to it, for many years, that's a good sign. Write it down, put it on your short list.

You'll need to sign up for Morningstar's premium subscription to use their filter, but it's well worth the investment if you're managing your investments on your own. If that's the case, you'll most likely come to rely on the wealth of information there, and your subscription will pay for itself many times over.

A Family of Funds

We've made good progress in figuring out what separates the good funds from the bad. But still, when we're starting with more than 20,000 funds to choose from, isn't there some way to narrow the field before we go bleary-eyed reading prospectuses?

Of course there is. Instead of scrutinizing a universe of mutual funds, and picking the ones you like one fund at a time, you can focus on clusters of funds called "families." A "family of funds" is a collection of mutual funds managed by a single investment firm. Each fund in the family may be managed by different professionals, but they're all under the oversight of the investment firm's management team, committee, or board of directors. As a result, they often reflect a similar strategy or investment style. For example, there are families of funds that are devoted to socially responsible investments. These families invest in companies that adhere to certain social, ethical, religious, or environmental standards. They may, for example, avoid tobacco companies. Other families are geared toward a particular investment philosophy. One might take the "guru" approach (see Chapter Eight, "Two Questions = Four Investment Strategies," starting on page 86) and search for hot stocks to add to its funds in an effort to time the market, while another opts for a more balanced approach to draw on different types of companies within each asset class. Currently there are more than 600 families to choose from.[37] If you find a family that mirrors your personal values and investment philosophy, it can

---

37   Here's a list offered by TD Ameritrade: https://research.tdameritrade.com/grid/
public/mutualfunds/fundfamilies/fundfamilies.asp?tab=families.

offer you a chance to stay within those parameters without having to research each fund one at a time.

But there are several other factors to consider before you decide whether to go with a family of funds or hand-pick from the greater universe of funds. And there are pros and cons on both sides of the issue.

One of the greatest benefits of a family of funds is that they generally allow you to buy and sell within their own selection of mutual funds without charging fees for each transaction. You may pay a fee to get in or out of the family, but once you're in, you're in. That means you can easily rebalance your portfolio without incurring transaction fees. They score high on the "ease of rebalancing" factor we looked at on page 149. For example, let's say the small-cap value section of your portfolio has a great year, and that portion of your portfolio increases in value so it's now 25% of your total investments, rather than the 14% you've targeted for your balanced, All-Weather Retirement Portfolio. You'll need to sell some of those stocks to bring that asset class back down to 14%. If you're in a family of funds, you won't pay a fee to move that money out of the small-cap value fund or into the others. But if you have different funds from different families, it will probably cost you.

The downside of a family of funds is that most don't offer funds in every asset class. You might find a fund that matches your values and investment style, with excellent offerings in the domestic market, but it doesn't offer an international fund. To be able to apply the worry-free investment philosophy, you must have all the basic areas covered, so you'd need to look elsewhere for that international fund—or find a different family.

Another drawback is that a fund in a particular asset class may be particularly weak, even though other funds in the same family look great. If you want to be in that family, you must be able to live with this one bad fund as part of the package, or miss out on the "ease of rebalancing" benefits.

Probably the greatest concern about families of funds, however, is the possibility they don't diversify within their family. For example, if all the funds are managed by one committee, they may have similar stocks in a lot of different funds. This would be devastating if the committee was wrong in their estimates of how those stocks would perform, because if they crash you'll feel the loss in several of your funds.

Picking from the universe of funds reduces that particular risk almost to nothing. When you choose individual funds on their merit, each from a different investment firm or family, each fund is managed by a different manager or management team with its own unique perspective. Avoiding families of funds also means you have more choices, so you can find the best fund in each category. If the fund changes managers, or just doesn't perform well, you can find another fund in that category.

The downside of picking from the universe of funds is that it can take a tremendous amount of time to make sure you don't have style drift. Another problem is that it's more difficult and much more costly to rebalance your portfolio. Remember our previous example, when your international stocks soared to 25% of the value of your portfolio? Chances are you'll incur fees to rebalance if you're not doing it within a fund family. Those fees can eat up the benefit of rebalancing.

What's more, it could take three to four days to shift money around between different families. If you rebalance quarterly, then you could be out of the market 12 days or more each year. That's enough to devastate your return if the market has a big swing on the days your money is in limbo.

Given the good and bad on both sides of the issue, I generally lean toward a family of funds—but with a twist. My approach is a hybrid that takes a little extra work. I like to invest primarily in a family, but also select a few outside funds where the family is particularly weak.

Stay tuned and I'll share some of my favorite families.

My Recommendations

As I've said, I personally prefer no-load funds. Brokers who work on commission, or who are compensated based on the number of transactions, tend to prefer loaded funds—because the load is where their commissions come from. People in academia, and advisors who work for a fee rather than on commission, tend to recommend no-load funds. I fall into the latter category. Still, there could be an exception, when using loaded funds might make sense. The only circumstance I can think of right now is if you had a trustworthy, knowledgeable friend who is an advisor and is compensated that way. Beyond that, it's your decision to make—just be sure to weigh the decision very carefully.

I have categorized my recommendations into three groups.

1. Loaded family of funds

2. Exchange-traded family of funds

3. No-load family of funds

All of the families listed here are well managed, are offered by solid companies with a proven track record, and offer all the asset classes you'll need to create your All-Weather Retirement Portfolio.

Loaded funds, if you have to

First, let me say it one more time: I don't like loaded funds. Never have. Since the brokers are getting paid the lion's share of their compensation up front, what incentive do they have to keep you happy and properly service your account?

That said, there's one company that sells more fund shares than any other mutual fund company, and it happens to sell loaded funds. That company is American Funds, and they seem to me to be the best of all the loaded funds out there. Their load decreases the more you invest, and they have low expense ratios. Also, when you rebalance your portfolio, as long as you stay within the American Funds family you won't need to pay a load each time you buy and sell, so the impact of being in a loaded fund isn't as great as it would otherwise be. The family does offer funds in every asset class you'd need to create your All-Weather Retirement Portfolio (to the best of my knowledge it's the only loaded family that does), so—in theory, at least—you could rebalance without incurring the added costs of paying the load. These funds do, however, have 12b-1 fees. (These are the hidden fees the investor has to pay to help market the funds. Why should you pay for that?) Their 12b-1 fees are reasonable, but remember, I don't like paying them at all.

Exchange-traded fund families

Exchange traded funds, or ETFs, are structured so they can be traded throughout the day. (Most mutual fund transactions take place at the end of the day.) They're among the types of funds that carry transaction fees, applied any time you buy or sell them, and those can add up if you need to rebalance frequently. Keep in mind, though, that transaction fees tend to be low (much lower than sales loads), advisors don't make commissions on them, and ETFs tend to have very low expense ratios. Also, they're designed not to have style drift, which minimizes the likelihood you'll eventually need to replace them to maintain the precise allocation of assets you're after.

Still, those transaction costs can add up quickly because, unlike sales loads, transaction fees apply even when you buy or sell funds within a single family. You'll need 6 funds to create your All-Weather Retirement Portfolio (see "The All-Weather Retirement Portfolio" on page 129 in Chapter Nine), and if you rebalance it quarterly and take monthly distributions, you could have as many as 96 transactions in a year.

With that in mind, currently there are three ETF families of funds that I like:

- iShares, a family of ETFs managed by BlackRock, Inc., a global investment management firm. www.iShares.com

- ETFs offered by Fidelity Investments, Inc., an American multinational financial services company. https://www.fidelity.com/etfs/overview

- ETFs offered by the Vanguard Group, an American investment advisory firm. https://investor.vanguard.com/etf

Between these three, you should be able to cover all your bases in each asset class to create your portfolio.

My favorite no-load fund families

The funds I like are those that offer sound management, a good track record for performance, a reasonable risk, and minimal cost in the form of load and expense ratio.

My favorite no-load fund families, in no particular order, are:

- Vanguard

- Dimensional Fund Advisors, or DFA

- SEI (Especially their Y-shares, which are a class of mutual fund shares designed for institutional investors, like those that manage mutual funds; Y-shares require a high minimum investment, but expense ratios and other fees are generally lower or even waived.)

- T. Rowe Price

- Fidelity

There is no such thing as a perfect fund family. Every one of them has its challenges. But these five are so strong in the areas that matter most, their benefits outweigh their shortcomings. I urge you to give them serious consideration.

We've covered a lot of ground in this chapter, and I understand it can be challenging to absorb and utilize it all. It's up to you to decide if you want to take on the challenge yourself, or enlist the help of a professional advisor. If you choose to manage your portfolio yourself, it's a big commitment. You'll need to develop a sound understanding of the funds you're in and, most importantly, you'll need to monitor them closely. If this sounds like something you want to do, and if you're up to the challenge, the information we've covered here will send you off in the right direction. If it sounds like more work than you want to take on at this stage in your life, best to put your energy into finding an advisor you can trust.

How do you find a trustworthy advisor? One who puts your interests first and wants to build a long-term relationship instead of selling you investment products?

Turn the page and I'll tell you how.

PART IV.

Ready to Set Sail

Chapter Twelve

Finding an Advisor You Can Trust

A few years ago, a college student interviewed me for a class assignment. Her task was to learn something about financial planning, and to ask tough questions about the industry in general.

Most of her questions were pretty basic: How should I start planning for retirement? How much should I save? What should I invest in? The usual drill. But then she launched the big question. It bothered me at the time, and for several days afterward. She asked, "What percentage of advisors out there would you recommend to your mom?"

I had to think long and hard about the answer. I had to acknowledge it was a short list. The truth is, I feel nauseous thinking about it now.

As I explained to the young woman, there are three primary things that she—and you—want from any trusted advisor. First, you want to be sure your advisor is very knowledgeable in the area in which you need help. In your case, finding someone who knows about investing for retirement is the right place to start. Second, you need to be able to trust him or her. Third, you want to be sure he cares about you.

There are many advisors out there who are knowledgeable, there are many who are trustworthy, and quite a few who actually care. The challenge is to find one who meets all three of those criteria.

I was rather pleased with this answer when I offered it to the young college student. But she wasn't satisfied. She persisted. "What percentage of advisors out there would you recommend to your mom? How many are qualified in all three areas?"

I squirmed. I didn't want to answer. I knew that my unvarnished, honest response would seem ... well ... negative. But I could see she wasn't going to let me off the hook. It's possible she didn't care as much as I did about the answer. For her, it was just a class project, and this was only one question on her list. What did it matter?

It mattered to me.

I answered, "Two percent."

"Only two? That's one in fifty! Why?" she asked.

"There are very few advisors who can meet all three standards." I replied.

And it's true. But does the average person on the street know how to find the one in fifty? Do you? Do you know what questions to ask?

In fact, given how tricky it is to find an advisor who meets all three criteria, should you even try? Or is it better and safer just to try to figure it all out yourself?

In this chapter we'll tackle that last question first. Then, in case you decide you do in fact want to hire an advisor, I'll give you the key questions you must ask before you hire one. Finally, I'll give you a scorecard you can use to rate potential advisors. It will make it much easier to see who measures up—and who doesn't.

Do You Really Need an Advisor?

Before you start interviewing advisors, ask yourself, "Do I really need one?" If you've made it this far into the material in this book, you now know enough about investing to realize how much there is to learn—with the likely conclusion that expert advice would itself be a good investment.

A great advisor will benefit you much more, over time, than he costs. Here are some of the critical things he can help you do:

- Allocate your assets in a way that's appropriate to your needs

- Rebalance your portfolio

- Monitor mutual funds

- Analyze your income disbursements (Will your money last as long as you do?)

- Save you time by helping you handle all these things

- Make decisions rationally rather than emotionally, and prevent you from making decisions based on emotion

- Prevent you from making The Big Mistake. The Big Mistake is the one you can't recover from—trying to hit the home run or time the market or find the hot stock and blowing it ... things that can cost you money you can't afford to lose at this stage of your life.

- Find and implement tax strategies appropriate to your situation (Most advisors, however, won't prepare your tax returns. For that you'll need to hire a tax professional like a CPA who specializes in tax preparation.)

- Develop estate tax strategies

- Provide advice and support, as needed, for your surviving spouse

Now, if you have the time, temperament, and talent to do all this, you may want to do it yourself. But expert assistance with *any one* item on the list can easily be worth the advisor's compensation.

Advisors, generally speaking, add value. There's a well-respected company called Dalbar, Inc., that specializes in providing research, analysis, and rankings to investment firms of all kinds. In 2007, Dalbar conducted a study that showed that the *average* advisor—not a star, mind you, just an average, middle-of-the-road kind of guy—will increase your investment income relative to what you would have done on your own. If all he does is help you keep *emotion* out of the decision-making process, that alone will probably earn his keep. That's because, of all of the things an advisor can do for you, what's most important is his ability to help you calm your nerves when times are tough and keep you grounded when things are great and you want to invest more aggressively. He helps you stick to the plan, which increases the probability that no matter what happens in the outside world, you will have a worry-free income for life.[38]

But what if you can find an advisor who's not just average, but great at what he does? Imagine the possibilities. By asking the right questions you can find someone who meets all three of our criteria: He is knowledgeable, he's trustworthy, and he cares about you.

The Scenario You Want to Avoid

First, let's look at a real-life situation to see how things can go wrong when you *don't* adequately screen your advisor at the start.

---

38 For a great read on this topic and more, check out these two books: *Why Smart People Make Big Money Mistakes and How to Correct Them* by Gary Belsky and Thomas Gilovich, and *Simple Wealth, Inevitable Wealth* by Nick Murray.

Berty[39] was a very frugal woman. Rumor had it that she reused her paper towels. She'd been working with a financial advisor, but sensed that something was wrong with the way things were going with her money. She asked her son Joey, a CPA, to take a look at her portfolio, but he felt helpless. He could see his mother was in trouble, and considered talking to the advisor. But Joey felt uncomfortable because Berty's situation was to a large extent a result of the advisor's "help." Instead, Joey called me.

When Berty and her son came into my office she had just turned 65, and was in great health. She was very positive and optimistic about life in general, and I admired her upbeat attitude. She was going to need it.

The problem was she had lost most of her money with the last advisor—and it was the kind of loss that can't be made up. Not in her lifetime.

Her husband, Mark, had died when she was 60. They were financially set after years of saving. Her husband had taken care of all the financial matters, and when he passed away Berty depended on the advisor to take care of her finances.

Her income from her Social Security check and her pension was $890 per month. It wasn't great, but it was okay. When her husband died, she had a nest egg of about $810,000 from his retirement plan and his life insurance. It seemed like enough, especially since the house was paid for. She needed to be able to draw $40,000, or about 5%, from her portfolio each year to live on.

That nest egg should have been able to provide that—if the advisor had known how to diversify properly. It seems her advisor was one of the most dangerous kinds. It's probably not the kind you're

---

39   The situation is real, but the names and a few of the minor details have been changed.

thinking of—he was kind, caring, and honest. He just didn't know what he was doing.

I looked over the statements. Four years before, tech stocks had looked hot. So had growth stocks. In fact, growth stocks had had almost a ten-year run of looking great. The advisor had never seen a bad market. So he invested fairly heavily into growth stocks. But then came the dot-com bust, a perfect financial storm of sorts where tech stocks and growth stocks were concerned. When Berty's portfolio started going down, the advisor applied dollar cost averaging to put even more money into growth stocks.

The portfolio continued to go down, he continued to put more into growth and tech stocks, and she continued to take money out. When the value of her portfolio fell below $200,000, Berty called her son.

Now she faces life with $1,200 in the bank, and a fourth of what she had started with in her retirement fund. There is no way her portfolio can provide the kind of income Berty is used to—that $40,000 a year has become a 20% distribution stream. At the current rate of spending she will be broke in about 6 years. She worries about buying gifts for her grandchildren.

Berty is hoping to find someone who can help her, but her concept of what a financial advisor can do is slightly warped. The sad thing is there is fairly little anyone can do. She wants to continue taking out $40,000 annual income, and still somehow make up the loss in her principal. She's looking for miracles.

After a long and difficult talk, we explored realistic expectations, and the fact that she has some tough choices to make. If she wants to maintain her standard of living she will have to go back to work. With few marketable skills, it's a tough choice.

But the reality is this: if something doesn't change soon, she will be out of money, and probably end up living with her kids. It's a heartbreaking story.

Why did this happen?

In Berty's case the advisor took advice from magazines and from his corporate office. He trusted them. But magazines have magazines to sell, and financial corporations have financial products to sell.

I scrutinized three years' worth of Berty's statements, and concluded the advisor had been honest, and tried to do the right thing. He just didn't know how. To make matters worse, he *didn't know* he didn't know. And a financial advisor who tries to do what is right but doesn't know enough to see trouble ahead is a very dangerous advisor indeed.

Why do I share this with you? Because you are probably not as watchful for this type of advisor as you need to be. You know there are rogues out there who are more concerned with commissions than your situation. And you're certainly smart enough to know there are people who will flat-out steal your money. But chances are you believe that if someone cares about you and is fundamentally honest, he will do a good job. Unfortunately, if he doesn't know what he's doing, he could be the honest, caring captain of a sinking ship.

> The bottom line is this. *You* are responsible for your financial future, so you need to take charge.

The bottom line is this. *You* are responsible for your financial future, so you need to take charge. You must educate yourself at least enough to ask intelligent questions *and be able to recognize bad advice when you get it.*

The Questions You Must Ask Before You Hire an Advisor

I've put together a list of questions to help you evaluate any and all financial advisors according to my three essential criteria. First, let's review those criteria one more time, with a little more detail:

1. Is he an expert in your area of need?

    □ Experience (Does he have enough?)

    □ Credentials (What documentation can he provide that indicates other individuals or organizations think he's qualified?)

    □ Knowledge (Is he knowledgeable in the areas that are most important to you?)

    □ Continuing education (Is he committed to keeping up with the latest developments in the financial arena?)

2. Can you trust her?

    □ Independence (Does she have it?)

    □ Background check (Is she clean, or does she have a problematic history?)

    □ Fiduciary (Is she committed to putting your interests first?)

    □ Limitations (We all have them, but does she know what hers are?)

3. Does he care about you?

    □ Investment philosophy (Does it match yours?)

    □ Compensation (Does he have a vested interest in seeing you do well?)

    ▫ Workload (Is he overworked?)

Now let's go over the questions you need to ask to evaluate your prospective advisor for each criterion. More importantly, I'll explain the answers you'll get from someone who deserves your trust—and the ones that should send you heading for the door.

The guidelines and criteria in this chapter will give you an overview of the most essential qualities you need in an advisor, and some solid tools to help you identify them in candidates you're considering. But there's a lot more you can do to make sure you choose the best available professional to manage your retirement investments. That's why I developed a comprehensive, step-by-step process to help you do that. I've provided all the details in my book *The Worry-Free Retirement Guide to Finding a Trustworthy Financial Advisor*.

Choosing an advisor is one of the most important decisions you'll make as you secure your worry-free retirement. I invite you to use the information in that book to take a deeper look at how you can make sure it's also the *best* decision you'll make.

—*Randy*

I. Is he an expert in your area of need?

Experience

"How much financial planning and investment advisory experience do you have?"

As a rule of thumb, if you have $100,000 or more in investable assets, consider only planners who have been providing financial services for at least 5 years; 10 is better. It would be nice if the advisor has been around long enough to have *actually experienced* a major market downturn. Many young ones haven't.

Typically the market goes through a major slide every 3 to 5 years. But sometimes the good times last even longer. For example, the 1990s really didn't see a major downturn, so an advisor starting out at the beginning of the decade could have gone 10 years without having the value (and discomfort) of that experience. Toward the end of the first decade of the 2000s we saw a significant drop in the market, and new advisors earned their stripes as they learned to survive it (or didn't).

All that means is that you want an advisor who was in the thick of it through at least one major market downturn. If you're not sure when the last one was, look for someone who has been on the job for a minimum of five years. There may be good planners with less experience, but why take the chance? I was once an inexperienced planner (although my first full year was 1987, the year of Black Monday), and helped other planners and investors who knew even less than I did. My intentions were solid, but I always recommend finding someone who has experienced the bad times as well as the good when it comes to advising for a worry-free income.

Credentials

"What professional designations have you earned?"

Seek only those professionals who have earned *recognized* financial qualifications. Some credentials represent formal education in the field; others merely indicate an affiliation with a particular organization.

Education is an important ingredient for a well-qualified financial advisor. He should have *at least one* of the following credentials:

- CFP®: Certified Financial Planner™

- CPA: Certified Public Accountant with a PFS (Personal Financial Specialist) designation

That's my opinion—and, admittedly, I'm biased because I have both. However, just because I'm biased, it doesn't mean I'm wrong.

It's also my opinion that a CFP® is the more important designation of the two, but both are great. Yes, there are many other quality designations, but these are the two I consider most important. The organizations that grant these designations require applicants to pass an initial exam and obtain continuing professional education. A planner with one or more of these credentials has made a commitment to a minimum amount of continuing education, or he can't keep the designation.

A college degree, and preferably an MBA (master of business administration) with an emphasis in finance, is also nice. Just like the professional designations, it does not prove competence, but it does indicate an ability to use analytical skills required in this profession. It suggests a good foundation for the professional courses and continuing education studies.

Be aware, too, that some designations are virtually meaningless. There are close to 200 different designations and letters financial planners can attach to their names. No wonder people are confused. A large brokerage company has recently come under fire for creating their own designation just to make their brokers look better. Beware!

And, of course, you need to confirm all designations and degrees by calling the organizations that confer them. Beginning on page 185, near the end of this chapter, you'll find a summary of the alphabet soup of designations, and phone numbers for the regulatory bodies that govern them. It's a handy resource, and if you make good use of it, it will protect you from making a bad hire.

Knowledge

You should also ask questions that will allow the advisor to demonstrate he has some basic knowledge about matters that are most crucial to you at this point in your life. For example, a great question to ask if you're about to retire is, *"What is section 72(t), and how does it apply to me?"* Section 72(t) of the Internal Revenue Code reveals how you can take money out of IRAs and avoid the 10% penalty (even if you're younger than 59½). Any retirement advisor worth his salt will know this code and what it can do for you.

Another good question is, *"I understand how dollar cost averaging helps people accumulate wealth. How does it affect me, now that I'm taking income out on a regular basis?"* If you've read Chapter Five, "Investing for Income Is Different," you know the right answer to this question.

Or you can ask, *"What are the mandatory distribution rules?"* The mandatory distribution rules are tax laws that say you must take a certain percentage out of your retirement account starting at age 72. If you don't take it out, you are penalized 50% (yes, you read that right—you lose half) of what you should have taken out. You want an advisor who's knowledgeable about this.

Continuing education

"How do you keep up with the constantly changing financial environment?"

In other words, how many hours of continuing education does he take? If he takes the minimum, how is he going to be better than the other advisors? You want him to say he takes around 50 or more hours (clock hours) of course work a year.

But just logging course hours isn't really enough. Get details. *"What are some of the courses you've taken?"* And, *"Are they related to retirement?"* *"Do you teach classes on the topic?"* Students will keep him on his toes. *"Are you studying for an advanced degree?"* *"Do you subscribe to financial publications other than general media?"* Reading trade journals, as opposed to *Newsweek* or *The Wall Street Journal*, is one more way to stay tuned in to the things he needs to know to advise you properly.

Let me assure you, these are important questions. There is no way on earth anyone can be excellent at planning unless he or she is committed to staying current on financial issues.

II. Can you trust her?

Independence

Independence is critical! It's an issue that goes to trust, as well as to whether or not this advisor cares about you. You shouldn't have to worry if she is doing what's best for her or her company, or for you.

The question to ask is, *"Are you an agent or a representative of one primary company?"*

If the answer is yes, you need to ask some follow-up questions. *"Then help me understand, how can you provide unbiased advice if you are an agent or a representative of one company?"* Listen to the answer. Does it sound reasonable? Does she tell you her company is the best at everything? Beware. Remember, if you go to a Volkswagen dealership looking for a car, they are probably going to recommend a Volkswagen no matter what your needs are. On the other hand, if she says something like, "Our products aren't the best in every category, certainly. But they are excellent in most, and I can stay on top of them if there is a problem. If they aren't excellent, then I will suggest some outside investments that are. Fair enough?" Even this answer isn't great, but it's okay. I might not let the issue be a deal breaker.

Ask, *"Does your firm sell any of its own products?"* This is a killer for most brokers. Beware of those whose first priority is to move their company's products! Many firms require their representatives to offer company products first, even if a better investment is available. In fact, in some cases in-house products are the only options they can recommend. *"Do you make more compensation selling the company's products than non-company products?"* As you know, compensation can come in many forms besides cash. Exotic trips to pretty places come to mind. Find out about any bonuses offered to top sellers of those in-house investment products.

Here's another one to ask: *"Are you required to meet a quota of a particular product?"* Many companies require a certain volume of product line to be sold. Even if the advisor is basically an honest person, if she has quotas to meet it puts a lot of pressure on her to sell certain things, regardless of whether or not they are appropriate for you.

If the answer to any of these last three questions is yes, then you don't need to ask the other questions. Move on to the next advisor.

Let me repeat: *Independence is critical.*

Background check

This isn't really a question, but it *is* a requirement. These days, it is a good idea to check with the regulatory authorities like the Securities and Exchange Commission (SEC, www.sec.gov, 800-SEC-0330) for advisors, and the Financial Industry Regulating Authority (FINRA, www.finra.org, 301-590-6500; formerly National Association of Securities Dealers, or NASD) for registered representatives. The FINRA website has a nice "BrokerCheck" button on its home page that allows you to check out the registered representatives in your area. There are also state securities agencies for registered representatives or advisors who work on a smaller scale, and state insurance regulators who license insurance agents. If you google your state's name, along with "department of securities" or "department of insurance," you'll find contact information for the appropriate regulating agencies where you can verify credentials and check for complaints or violations.

It's tough for any professional to deal with the general public for 10 years and not have any complaints, but you want to be aware if your planner has been found guilty of felonies or is not currently licensed. (Don't laugh. We've seen it happen.)

I used to suggest asking for at least three client references. However, the reality is the advisor you're considering will give you her best clients, the ones who think their advisor walks on water. Ask, if you want, but don't put a lot of weight on it.

Fiduciary

A fiduciary is someone who, by law, must put your interests first instead of her own or those of the company she works for. This must be an absolute requirement for any advisor you hire.

Ask, *"Are you a fiduciary on all accounts, including retirement accounts and taxable accounts?"* You want an emphatic "Yes!" As of this writing, there are pending changes in the federal laws regarding fiduciaries; states have their own regulations, and some states have higher standards than others. But whether it's legally required or not, you need an advisor who is a fiduciary on all accounts. If the answer to this question is "No," this is not the advisor for you.

If you do get a positive response, ask, *"Can you send me something stating in writing that you are a fiduciary?"* The advisor must be willing to send you a written statement via email, fax, or regular mail. Nothing else here will do.

Your objective here, though, is twofold. You're looking for the appropriate answer to your question, of course. But this is also a way to find out if the advisor will follow up and do what she says she is going to do (send you the fiduciary disclosure). If she doesn't follow up in the initial honeymoon stage, she's unlikely to do it down the road.

Once you receive the documentation from the advisor, you'll need to verify it. You can do that by verifying she has credentials that require her to act as a fiduciary. If the advisor is a registered investment advisor (RIA) or an investment advisor representative (IAR), government entities require it. If she is a Certified Financial Planner™ (CFP°) or a member of the National Association of Professional Financial Advisors (NAPFA), her professional organization's code of conduct requires it. Refer to "Financial Advisor Alphabet Soup" on page 185 for information on all these designations and how to verify them.

Limitations

"Which outside professionals do you bring in, and when do you bring them in?"

You need to be able to trust the person you hire to know her limitations and to call on other experts as the need arises. Being surrounded by a diverse and savvy team is the mark of a smart advisor. No individual can be an expert in all the areas that affect your portfolio—investing, tax laws, asset protection, insurance, estate tax laws, and more. It's extremely tough to be at the top of her game in one area, much less all of them. Therefore, a good advisor has a team of one or more outside professionals—attorneys, accountants, insurance agents, pension experts, mortgage brokers, and so on. Working with these specialists on a regular basis will enable her to draw on their expertise to expand on her own knowledge base, and bring in the right help to optimize your investments and get you answers in a timely fashion.

III. Does he care about you?

Investment philosophy

"What is your investment philosophy?"

Before you sit down for an in-depth interview, take a few minutes to go over Chapter Eight, "The Two Most Important Questions," and review your personal investment philosophy. It's essential that you find an advisor whose philosophy agrees with yours. Does he try to pick the "hot stock of the week"? Does he try to time the market? Does he claim he can get a big return with no risk? (This can't be done. If he says he can … *run!*) Or is he a prudent, long-term investor who applies sound principles of asset allocation? The advisor should have a consistent, conservative investment philosophy that does not confuse investing with trading or speculating. He should have a proven, effective record in good years as well as bad, under all types of economic and political conditions, indicating he has a *disciplined* philosophy—not one that's influenced by the latest trend making the rounds on investment blogs.

Once you've established that the advisor is on the same page as you regarding investment philosophy, he should be willing to implement it in the following ways:

- For all the reasons we've outlined in this book, your advisor should construct your portfolio according to an allocation similar to the All-Weather Retirement Portfolio we developed in Chapter Nine, "Ten Steps to a Worry-Free Income for Life."

That means, to reduce overall volatility, the portfolio should be constructed with different investment areas (asset classes) that have dissimilar movement in different economic situations. If your advisor deviates greatly from this philosophy, you should ask and understand why.

- The advisor should discuss with you the expected rates of return for your portfolio, and what it will look like in the perfect financial storm scenario. That way, if stormy economic times do roll in, you'll be prepared.

- He should show you different models and mixes of investments that have the highest probability of achieving your goals.

- The advisor should be willing and able to purchase the selected asset classes with *institutional no-load* mutual funds, those that are typically available only to pension plans, large investors, and the like. These funds have everything you need—low expense ratios, no loads, generally no style drift, and so forth—but they also usually require higher minimum investments. However, if the advisor has a lot of money under his management, he can unlock the door to these funds for an average, non-institutional investor like yourself. It's one of the perks you can get by working with a professional.

- The advisor should be prepared to rebalance your portfolio periodically. The rebalancing decisions should be considered in terms of cost and tax consequences.

- Finally, the advisor should be willing to put all these elements in writing in an investment policy statement. This statement should provide specific instructions and cover such topics as target rates of return, risk tolerance, what percentage of the portfolio will be held in each asset class, and rebalancing.

Compensation

"How do you get paid?"

No one works for free. Financial advisors get paid, primarily, in one of two ways. Either they get paid on commission every time they buy or sell a stock or bond or other investment vehicle, or they get paid a fee that's either an hourly rate or an annual amount based on the size of your portfolio. Commissions are paid by the company the advisor works for. A fee is paid by the client. Right from the start, that should give you some indication of where an advisor's loyalties are likely to be.

A fee-based advisor is usually paid a percent of the assets under their management, between 0.9% and 1.5% per year (or less, depending on the amount of assets you have; the larger your portfolio, the smaller your fee percentage is likely to be). With this compensation method the planner does better when you do better, because when your assets increase, his income increases. It also works the other way—when the value of your account drops, his income goes down. This method fosters a long-term relationship with the client. The longer your advisor keeps you happy, the better he does. He doesn't make all his compensation on the front end. Think about it: You bring your money to the advisor, and he invests it for you. Those initial investments generate lots of commissions if that's how he's getting paid. Not so with a fee-based advisor. He gets his 1.25%, more or less—that's it. Generally, he must keep you happy as a client for approximately 5 years to break even compared to the commissioned advisor. So a fee advisor wants you to stick with him for the long haul, and therefore has a vested self-interest in doing a great job for you.

That's what you want.

There are also fee-only advisors who work on an hourly basis. This is sometimes difficult for the advisor because he is constantly being asked if he really did spend the time he billed out for, and if he is worth his hourly rate. Attorneys have the same problem. But from a client's perspective, this is usually a good way to pay an advisor. If you trust him, don't rake him over the coals every time you get an invoice.

If the advisor doesn't charge fees, he is probably on commission, making money from the sale of products. This is a potential conflict of interest. If one product offers more commission or a better trip or more company perks, it can influence an advisor's recommendations. He may not even realize his judgment is being swayed. If he is purely commission based, making all his compensation up front, you should be cautious. If he isn't charging fees, ask, *"Since you make money on transactions, help me understand how I can be sure I get advice that's in my best interest."* You might give him the benefit of the doubt if he says something like, "I've been in business for 15 years, and most of my business comes from referrals, like yourself. I have never had a complaint, and I couldn't have been in business this long, or receive that many referrals, if I didn't do what is best for my clients." But if he starts to fidget, or won't look you in the eye, it's a bad sign.

Here's another reason why this issue is so important. If an advisor is getting paid by commission and not by fees, usually he gets paid a large chunk on the front end of each transaction and almost nothing (or exactly nothing) to service the client (you). Ongoing service is critical: Reviewing your portfolio to make sure you are on track, rebalancing the portfolio, answering your questions promptly, taking care of issues that come up, keeping you up to speed on the tax laws, making sure your estate plan is up to date, and so forth. How is he going to feed his family and properly service the client relationship if he makes next to nothing to service his clients? He either has to "churn" the client (buying and selling investments to generate commissions) or continue to beat the bushes to bring in new clients (and not see the existing ones). Do you see the problem?

There's another twist to this discussion. Some advisors charge a fee *and* earn commissions on sales. So even if you know you're interviewing someone who'll ask you to pay a fee, ask, *"Do you also make commissions on products you recommend?"* If he says, "Yes," this should not necessarily be taken as a negative response. However, you should recognize the potential conflict of interest. There are financial companies that charge a small fee to do a canned or generic financial plan, knowing they will make a large profit selling their products. You can try to circumvent this by asking, *"Can I implement the plan on my own?"* If the planner squirms, it is probably at the thought of losing the commission. Beware.

Don't get me wrong. There are some advisors working on commission who are excellent, who do not let the potential conflict of interest influence their recommendations. In fact, there are even some I would recommend to my mom. They are just harder to find than the ones working for fees.

The bottom line is that you need to know if an advisor's priorities are aligned with yours, and whether his approach is "client driven," which means your needs are the priority, or "product driven," which means they're not. As we've seen, fee-only advisors are usually client driven, while commission advisors are generally driven by the products they want to sell.

You can dig a little deeper by asking, *"How do you analyze a situation, and what process do you use to make recommendations?"* If his approach is client driven, he should first find out how you feel about your situation. He should understand your goals and what you're trying to accomplish. Then, he should get a detailed understanding of your income, assets, debts, company benefits, and so forth. Finally, he will work up an action plan that addresses your concerns and gives you solutions. Ideally the plan should include several different suggestions that address your concerns, with the pros and cons of each choice.

If instead he starts out by telling you how a particular investment will serve your needs without finding out about you, and what your needs really are, then you are probably in the office of someone pushing products. The last thing you want at this time of your life is to fall victim to a good product salesman. There is nothing wrong with investing in financial products, as long as they fit *your* needs, and not just those of the salesperson.

A good financial plan may be many things. It can be a list of action steps on a legal pad, all the way up to a thick set of charts and graphs. One is not necessarily better than the other. It depends on how detailed your needs are and what kind of experience your advisor has. Even if the written plan is short, the advisor's fact-finding about you should be thorough. If you're about to retire, the planner should ask you about your retirement income needs, look at your tax return, talk about risk and how you feel about it, show you some portfolios, talk about estate planning, and more. In other words, he asks about *a broad range* of financial issues—not just the ones he can make money on.

Workload

"How many clients do you have, and how many new ones do you take on every year?"

Does this advisor care about you? Maybe he means to, but it is impossible for anyone to handle a thousand clients with a high level of personal service.

It's true that a given advisor may be able to handle a larger client load than most. It depends on his personality, staff, resources, and business systems setup, the outside professionals available to him, and many other factors. A competent and experienced team that works closely together can be more effective than a single superstar or a big, loosely knit organization. Find out how fast the advisor can respond to your needs. Make sure you will be getting excellent service and advice, and that you won't be just a number in a planner's overloaded schedule.

That leads us to the next question: *"How often will we meet to review my financial situation?"* You should be able to meet with the advisor, face to face, at least annually, preferably semi-annually, and in the best situations quarterly. This depends on the amount you have invested and the complexity of your financial situation. You should also be able review your investment performance on a quarterly basis, with printed reports that include comparisons to appropriate benchmark performances.

You should also ask, *"What happens if something comes up? Do I have to wait until it's time for our periodic review to discuss it?"* Things happen. You don't want to wait 6 months to get an answer to a question that's important to you. You should be able to call and ask, without an additional charge.

Termination fees

"What happens if it doesn't work out?"

There's one more question you must ask—it may be more important than any of the others, and it's this: *"What happens if I'm not happy with your services?"*

The benefits you receive from hiring an advisor should outweigh the cost. In case they don't, ask, *"What are the charges and fees if I want to get out of this arrangement?"* If you are unhappy, does it cost you 5% to 10% of your portfolio to get out? (We've seen even larger numbers!) Be careful. Know your options. A relatively small fee—say $200 or less—is common. But it doesn't make sense to me to pay a large "get out" fee, as my dad would call it. If you're not happy, you should be able to leave without getting hammered with costs. If an advisor uses fees as coercion to keep you as a client, it should send up a serious red flag.

I believe investments are like countries. If a country has to have a wall to keep its people in, it's not a good country. If an investment—or an investment advisor—has hefty surrender charges, then it's probably not a good investment.

Begin Your Search

There you have it: all the questions you need to ask an advisor to determine if he or she is right for you. It's true that some of these questions are tough to ask—you may be concerned about insulting the planner. However, I can't stress it enough: *Do not hesitate to ask each and every one of these important questions.* We are talking about *your* money here, and your future. Don't put it at risk because you're reluctant to get the information you need. You must *not* be shy. If you feel too embarrassed to ask the questions, have a trusted friend or relative ask for you. Just be sure to *get these questions asked and answered!*[40]

Why am I so insistent about this? Because getting the right help is so important. I want you to have an advisor I would recommend to my mom, someone who falls into that elite 2%—someone who's

---

40   For a printable script that includes these questions and much more, see my book *The Worry-Free Retirement Guide to Finding a Trustworthy Financial Advisor*. PDF versions of the script are also available on my website at www.RandyThurman.com.

knowledgeable, someone you can trust, someone who cares about you. Anything less could spell disaster for your financial future.

To help streamline the process for you, I've included a Financial Advisor Scorecard on page 189, at the end of this chapter. Make a copy of it and use it as you evaluate prospective advisors.

> I want you to have an advisor I would recommend to my mom.

Financial Advisor Alphabet Soup

"What do all those letters really mean?"

The following is a glossary of credentials and affiliations you'll run across as you search for a financial advisor you can trust. I've included contact information you can use to verify whether the advisor you're considering has in fact earned and maintained the right to use a given credential as he claims.

CDFA™: Certified Divorce Financial Analyst. The Institute for Divorce Financial Analysts (IDFA) is the premier national organization dedicated to the certification, education, and promotion of the use of financial professionals in the divorce arena. It requires three years of experience and competence level on exams. Contact: www. InstituteDFA.com, (800) 875-1760.

CFA: Chartered Financial Analyst. This is a fairly prestigious credential held primarily by institutional money managers and stock analysts. It is issued after several years of appropriate work experience and rigorous testing by the Association for Investment Management and Research in Charlottesville, Virginia. Contact: www.CFAinstitute.org, (800) 247-8132.

CFP®: Certified Financial Planner™. The credential is issued by the Certified Financial Planner Board of Standards in Washington, DC, a nongovernmental organization. An applicant must complete five topic-specific exams and then a comprehensive exam, and agrees to abide by a code of ethics. A person who has a CFP® is serious about the profession. Out of all the designations, this is the one I would recommend as most essential for the advisor you ultimately hire. Contact: www.CFP.net, (800) 487-1497.

ChFC: Chartered financial consultant. This designation is issued by The American College of Financial Services in King of Prussia, Pennsylvania. I generally see CLUs (see below) take a few additional courses and receive this designation. Although it is intended to indicate more of a financial planning background, the coursework seems to me to be heavily insurance based. Contact: Visit the website sponsored by The American College of Financial Services at www.DesignationCheck.com/advisor-search, or call (888) 263-7265.

CLU: Chartered Life Underwriter. This designation is issued by The American College of Financial Services in King of Prussia, Pennsylvania, and is probably the most respected designation for insurance expertise. This designation is held mostly by life insurance agents. CLUs sign a code of ethics, have experience in the field, and have completed five required classes and three elective classes. By taking additional courses, an agent can obtain a ChFC certificate, also issued by The American College. Contact: www.DesignationCheck.com/advisor-search, (888) 263-7265.

CPA: Certified Public Accountant. A CPA must pass an extensive, rigorous test administered nationally, and receive approval from state accountancy boards. CPAs are trained to work in many areas. Generally, the ones that can help you plan your retirement investments will also have the PFS designation (see below). This is a designation specifically for CPAs helping clients in the area of personal financial planning. To confirm that a CPA has an active license, go to: www.CPAverify.org. Or, for more research options, you can contact the appropriate State Board of Accountancy where the individual obtained his or her license. There is a complete list of contact information for each state board located at this website address: www. AICPA.org/Advocacy/State/StateContactInfo/Pages/StateContactInformation.aspx. Click on the state, then click on the link to that state's accountancy board website. Each site should have a link that says, "Find a CPA," or something similar.

CPA/PFS: Certified Public Accountant/Personal Financial Specialist. The Personal Financial Specialist (PFS) program allows CPAs to demonstrate their knowledge and expertise in personal financial planning. CPA/PFS credential holders have specific experience, education, and examination requirements that set them apart from other CPAs and financial planners. This is a really outstanding designation. To find one in your area, go to www.AICPA.org, type "Find a CPA/PFS" in the search box, and click the link. Or if you prefer, call the AICPA at (888) 777-7077.

IAR: Investment Advisor Representative. See RIA.

MBA: Master of business administration. This graduate-level degree is generally seen as an indication of a solid background in financial matters. Call the university indicated on the advisor's degree to confirm its validity.

NAPFA: National Association of Personal Financial Advisors. NAPFA is the country's leading professional association of fee-only financial advisors—highly trained professionals who are committed to working in the best interests of those they serve. The organization has been helping people find fee-only advisors since 1983. Contact: www.NAPFA.org, (888) 333-6659 (or 888-FEE-ONLY).

RIA: Registered Investment Advisor. Not a credential, it simply means an individual or a firm has submitted certain filings with the SEC, the individual has passed an exam, paid a modest fee, and is held to a higher standard of responsibility and accountability. An advisor who works in an RIA firm is called an "investment advisor representative," or IAR. An RIA, an RIA firm, or an IAR is a fiduciary and required to put the client's interests first. In my opinion you should always use an RIA or an IAR. To verify an advisor is registered and in good standing, go to www.AdviserInfo.sec.gov/IAPD/Content/Search/iapdSearch.aspx.

RR: Registered representative. This refers to a person who has passed one or more securities exams, and who is regulated by the Financial Industry Regulatory Authority, more commonly known as FINRA. There is no explicit financial-planning component to the testing. *This is also not a professional designation* but part of the licensing required *to sell* securities on a commission basis. Unfortunately the exams cover a lot of stuff most advisors will never use in a lifetime in the securities business. They're difficult tests, but the knowledge base they cover is so very broad that it is probably not going to help you in the areas most important to you. FINRA maintains a database of all licensees, any complaints that have been lodged against them, and how those complaints have been resolved. In some cases complaints are minor, or the agency has determined a complaint was unfounded. In any case, it's a good idea to check. Contact: www.FINRA.org, (301) 590-6500.

Financial Advisor Scorecard™

1. **Ask: "How many years of financial planning experience do you have?"**

   1 point per year, up to 10 points.

2. **Ask: "How many hours of continuing education do you take per year?"**

   1 point for every 5 hours, up to 10 points.

3. **Ask: "What are your professional designations?"**

   5 points for each of the following: CPA, CPA/PFS, CFP®, ChFC, up to 10 points.

4. **Ask: "Are you a registered investment advisor?"**

   10 points if Yes, minus 10 if No.

5. **Ask: "Do you have college degrees that help you? What are they?"**

   10 points for master's, 6 points for bachelor's, 3 points for associates. Maximum 10 points.

6. **Ask: "What is code section 72(t)?" (Tests knowledge of an important retirement tax law.)**

   10 points if very knowledgeable, 3 if somewhat knowledgeable.

7. **Ask: "Do you offer a free initial consultation?"**

   5 points if Yes.

8. **Ask: "Does your firm offer proprietary (company) products?"**

   10 points if No, minus 5 if Yes.

9. **Ask: "How are you compensated?"**

   10 points if fee only, 3 if fee and commission.

10. **Call State Securities department or, if appropriate, the SEC. Have any complaints been filed against the advisor?**

    10 points if No, 5 if Yes but minor.

11. **In the initial consultation, was the advisor open and honest about his or her compensation method without you asking?**

    5 points if Yes.

12. **What is the advisor's investment philosophy? Does it match yours?**

    If you do not have a match, automatic disqualification.

13. **Ask: "Will you act as a fiduciary on my account? If so, will you put that in writing?"**

    If No, automatic disqualification.

14. **In the initial consultation, did the advisor listen to your goals and concerns?**

    If No, automatic disqualification.

15. **In the initial consultation, was the advisor client driven (and not product driven)?**

    If No, automatic disqualification.

16. **Do you feel comfortable with the advisor?**

    If No, automatic disqualification.

17. **Bonus points: Advisor or firm has been named a top advisor by a national publication or by his or her peers.**

    10 points per award, 20 maximum.

18. **Bonus points: Advisor has more than 30 years' professional experience, specializes in retirement investing and has done extensive research on retirement portfolios, is a CPA/PFS and a CFP®, has an MBA, and is a published author who has written a book on the All-Weather Retirement Portfolio.**

    100 points, double if advisor's initials are R.L.T.

Total Points: _____

100 points possible before the bonus.

Grade like a school paper: 90–100 is an "A," 80–89 is a "B," and so on.

Chapter Thirteen

Make Your All-Weather Retirement Portfolio Even Sunnier

The All-Weather Retirement Portfolio we've developed throughout the pages of this book is based on in-depth analysis of various market conditions since 1930, more than two thousand pages of spreadsheets, and hundreds (maybe thousands?) of hours of research. I've compiled all that data and research, along with my 35-plus years of experience, to generate a formula you can use to create your own investment plan—or work with an advisor to do so—with confidence that it will provide you with a worry-free income for the rest of your life.

But as with most things in life, the best formula in the world is subject to tweaks and nuances that reflect your own interests and concerns. And, the reality is that my experience has taught me some things that go beyond the hard data. So, before I send you off to apply the principles we've discussed, I'd like to share a few enhancements I think you'll find interesting. You already have all the information you need to chart a course that will carry you safely through that perfect financial storm, should it arise during your retirement years. Now, let's trim the sails a bit, so you can fine-tune that course into your future.

Go beyond the Research

The portfolio we put together in Chapter Nine, "Ten Steps to a Worry-Free Income for Life," includes six asset classes. For most of those, we have more than 85 years of data available to evaluate their historical performance and how each type of investment is likely to perform throughout the years of your retirement. I used that historical performance to show you how those assets would perform when combined in a diversified portfolio, so that together they mitigate the impact of the worst financial times you're likely to encounter in the next 40 years. It's a strong portfolio that you can count on for a worry-free retirement income. It also has the advantage that, with just six asset classes, you can create a similar portfolio and manage it on your own.

But the fact is, when I create portfolios for my own clients I go beyond the research to make a few enhancements based on my personal experience as an investor and advisor. I've developed a more complicated formula that distributes assets among not six, but nine different asset classes. Some of the additional investment vehicles haven't been around long enough to generate a measurable track record through financial hard times. Still, by applying fundamental principles of diversification, and seeking out investments that perform differently under similar circumstances, I've found a way to make a very good portfolio even better.

With nine different asset classes, it would be more challenging for you to create and manage this enhanced portfolio on your own. But if you're working with an advisor, I encourage you to share it with him or her, and consider using it as the basis for your investment strategy.

Diversify the Bond Portion of Your Portfolio

Since it works so well to diversify the stock or equity portion of your portfolio, as we did in Chapter Nine, "Ten Steps to a Worry-Free Income for Life," it makes sense to diversify the bond side as well. There are three bond, or debt, areas that I recommend to improve diversification: international bonds, emerging market debt, and high-yield bonds. Unfortunately, since there is limited historical data documenting how these markets have performed, I can't run these asset classes through the Perfect Financial Storm Test to demonstrate unequivocally why this is a smart move—that's why I didn't include it in the basic All-Weather Retirement Portfolio. Hopefully those data will become available in the coming years. What I can offer you today is my decades of experience, which includes a deep understanding of how these markets work—and I've seen how this strategy has benefited my clients over the years.

First, I recommend placing between 30% and 50% of your bonds in international debt. International bonds are issued by governments and by companies in countries other than the United States. Strangely enough, the return on international bonds is almost the same as that of US bonds. (This may suggest what the world market thinks of the risk of US debt as compared to other developed countries. But that's a discussion for another book ...) Even so, you'll still see the benefits of diversification because you reduce your sensitivity to the fluctuations of US interest rates. Actually, with a diversified bond portfolio, you decrease your specific exposure to *any single* country's interest rate. If the interest rate in one country goes the wrong way, you're protected because you've spread your risk among several different countries. Lower interest-rate risk in this scenario translates to more dependable returns. Not bad.

As you might expect, there is a tradeoff. When you invest in international bonds you incur a new risk due to fluctuation in exchange rates. When you need your money, if the currency the bond is issued in is worth fewer dollars than when you bought it, your bond will effectively be worth less (but not worthless). While I generally don't like incurring a new risk, in this case I believe the benefits justify it.

As for finding quality mutual funds for international bonds, once again they're tough to find. I like SEI; Vanguard, Fidelity, and T. Rowe Price are also good.

Just as we did with your stocks, I recommend further diversifying your international bonds to include emerging market debt—again, from countries that are not yet considered developed countries, but do have their own currency (that is, the bonds are issued in a currency other than dollars). These are primarily issued by governments, not corporations. Emerging market countries that issue debt include:

- Brazil

- South Africa

- Mexico

- Chile

- Fiji

- Peru

- Russia

In this area, like the equities, I recommend placing about 30% of your international bonds into emerging market debt.

For mutual funds in emerging market debt, I like only T. Rowe Price and SEI. That's it. It's really a tough area to find quality—and it's an area that needs to be expertly monitored.

Finally, I recommend you diversify the US portion of your bond portfolio into one more area: high-yield bonds. "High-yield bonds" is basically a euphemism for "junk bonds," because most people cringe at the idea of buying anything called "junk." Anyway, these bonds offer a high yield because they have a higher default risk. They carry a rating of BB or lower by Standard & Poor's, or Ba or lower by Moody's. Because of their high risk, you should *only* invest in these bonds through a mutual fund to reduce your risk.

You'll want to further protect yourself by buying only short- and intermediate-term bonds in this category. The average maturity should be 5 years or less. This decreases the interest rate risk with a minimal decrease in return. This is particularly important in the current economic environment of very low rates. You don't want to be locked into a low rate for a really long time, as you would be with a long-term bond.

Based on my experience, high-yield bonds should make up about 10% of your bond exposure, or 3% of your total portfolio.

The Final Portfolio

Here's the final portfolio, with all the enhancements we've discussed:
- 30% bonds (or debt)
  - 17% US short and intermediate term
  - 7% international
  - 3% emerging market
  - 3% high yield

- 49% US stocks

  - 23% large-cap value

  - 12% large-cap growth

  - 14% small-cap value

- 21% international stocks

  - 15% developed countries

  - 6% emerging markets

Optimize Your Distribution Strategy

This book is all about creating a portfolio that will provide you with a worry-free income for the rest of your life. But once you've generated that income stream, you have a lot of options regarding how you take the money out. The choices you make when it comes time to withdraw your money can also make a significant difference in how long your portfolio lasts and how much cash you have to spend.

> This book is all about creating a portfolio that will provide you with a worry-free income for the rest of your life.

Here are three strategies that will help you make the best decisions regarding your distributions:

- Take monthly distributions.

- Take money from each asset class.

- Minimize your tax exposure.

Take monthly distributions

The data analyses I've done throughout this book assume you'll take your distributions annually, at the beginning of each year. If you do that, though, that large chunk of money won't be generating returns for you while it's sitting in your checking account waiting for you to spend it. That may work to your advantage if it's a negative year, but it really hurts you in the positive years, which is the case a majority of the time. It's far better to take monthly distributions, so your money can remain in your All-Weather Retirement Portfolio and work for you for as long as possible.

Take money from each asset class

Each time you take a distribution, I recommend you take money from every asset class in your portfolio, on a pro-rata basis. This just means you'll use the percentage allocation you've identified as your target for each segment of your portfolio to determine how much of your distribution you'll take from that asset class.

Minimize your tax exposure

As you probably know, when you withdraw money from an account there could be tax consequences. Different types of accounts are taxed at different rates, and in some cases they're tax free. So knowing which accounts to draw from can have a big impact on your tax liability. There are about as many techniques and strategies that apply here as there are vacation destinations to choose from (assuming you're not too fussy about travel plans—seriously, there are a ton of techniques and strategies), but I've identified two basic principles that will help you make smart choices:

- If you must pay a dollar in taxes, it's generally better to pay it at some time in the future than to pay it today. That way, that dollar will keep working for you for as long as possible in your All-Weather Retirement Portfolio.

- However, if you're in a lower tax bracket, it makes sense to take ordinary income out of taxable retirement accounts up to the amount that's taxed at the lowest tax rates. It's a way to reduce the amount of money that might be subject to a higher tax rate in the future.

Let's look at some examples.

If you're in a mid to high tax bracket, and you can take money from a Roth IRA or a traditional IRA, I recommend taking it from the Roth, because that money is not taxable. It's true, you'll take the tax hit later on if you start drawing money from the traditional IRA—all of which is taxable, because you didn't pay taxes on it when it went into the account. But the money you save on taxes will remain in your account earning money for you until you really need it, which has the effect of reducing your net loss from those tax payments.

Here's how that pencils out in real dollars. Let's say you have $100,000 in that traditional IRA and $100,000 in the Roth. You have other income that puts you in the 33% tax bracket, but you'd also like to take a 5% distribution ($10,000 total) from your retirement accounts. (We'll assume you're over 59½, have had the Roth for more than 5 years, and you're younger than 72 so you're not subject to the required minimum distribution, or RMD, from your traditional IRA.) Many people choose to take the money from the conventional IRA, even though that distribution is taxable, in hopes of reducing the amount they'll be forced to take out later when they *are* subject to the RMD. However, if instead you take the $10,000 out of the Roth, and do the same thing for the next 10 years, you still should have some nice money left in the Roth (assuming your investments there made some money, which is extremely likely). At the same time, the balance in your traditional IRA will then be about $200,000 (assuming a 7.2% return)—and you will have saved about $33,000 in taxes,[41] which of course has continued to earn money for you over the years.

But what if you're in, say, the 12% tax bracket? And what if your income is low enough that you could add another $10,000 before you enter the next bracket, which is 22%? In that case I'd like to see you max out that 12% bracket by taking $10,000 from a taxable account, like a traditional IRA or 401(k). That way, when you reach the age when you're subject to the required minimum distribution, the balance in your taxable account will be lower than if you hadn't taken that money out, so you're less likely to take that RMD hit in a higher tax bracket. If you don't need the cash, you can "convert" the money by putting it into a Roth IRA, so it'll keep earning money for you—all of which will be tax free when you do take it out.

It's All about the Sunshine

My last—and maybe my best—piece of advice is this: Enjoy your retirement.

That's what this book is all about: providing you a steady stream of retirement income; showing you how to weather the storms— and yes, they will come—maximizing the cash in your pocket while making sure, as much as you can, that you don't run out of money; helping you pay the least amount in taxes as the law will allow … all of this is designed to provide you a truly worry-free retirement. I've pored over mountains of data and invested countless hours to help you find the sweet spot, so you can spend your money on the things

---

41   These numbers are based on past performance, which is no guarantee of future performance. Although the returns used in this example represent reasonable assumptions, your actual return would undoubtedly be different.

that matter to you while you're able to, while you're healthy, and do so without guilt, and with confidence that your financial future is secure.

Yes, I know, it's not easy. However, there's a balance that makes it all possible, and with the information in this book you have the knowledge you need to find that balance. It's my hope that you'll use it to sail into your future with a peaceful heart, and reap all the benefits you so richly deserve.

Chapter Fourteen

The Eight Most Common Questions about the All-Weather Retirement Portfolio

We've covered a lot of ground since that initial conversation with Linda, who first came to see me when she was ready to retire and looking for options. We've gone over some basic principles of investing, and I've shown you a step-by-step approach to creating a portfolio that will provide you with a worry-free income for the rest of your life, even if you encounter that perfect financial storm. I've even shared some details about how I fine-tune that portfolio for my own clients, using strategies I've developed through my hard-earned experience.

But inevitably there are circumstances you'll encounter that are difficult to cover in the pages of a book, and concerns you'll have as you lie in bed some sleepless night. It's my guess that most of those issues have been brought to me by clients at one time or another, in an effort to make absolutely sure they have a plan that addresses their own unique needs and concerns. What follows are the questions I'm asked most often—and at least a few are probably on your mind, too. Let's go through them one by one so we can put your mind at ease.

Question #1. *"It's hard to believe any plan is as 'worry-free' as you say. There must be some hidden element that has the potential to blow it out of the water. What is it?"*

Without a doubt, the biggest "hidden element" is letting emotions override the plan. This can happen in both good years and bad. In the 1990s when everyone was making a killing in technology stocks and dot-coms, many investors were dissatisfied with their good returns, because they were inferior to those of other investors who were taking on the big risks of those up-and-coming dot-com equities. In fact, the most blistering criticism I've had as an advisor was on the back end of 1999 when I refused to go more heavily into tech stocks. I actually lost some clients over it. However, by 2000 when that big tech bubble finally popped, most everyone was very happy I'd avoided it—except, as you can imagine, those clients who left.

Of course, it also works the other way. When bad years hit—and if you're in the market long enough, they will—investors want to dump their stocks and switch to cash. Study after study shows that you can't time the market. But emotionally, we all want to.

> Study after study shows that you can't time the market. But emotionally, we all want to.

Emotions are the biggest enemy of this All-Weather Retirement Portfolio. You must stay the course, when things are going well and especially when they're not. The highest probability of success, in my opinion, is to simply stick to the plan and not deviate from it.

Question #2. *"Most plans for retirees seem to recommend a blend of 60% stocks and 40% bonds. But you recommend a 70/30 blend. Why?"*

It's true that many advisors recommend a 60/40 balance between stocks and bonds, typically 60% stocks and 40% long-term government bonds. We looked closely at a similar formula in Chapter Nine, "Ten Steps to a Worry-Free Income for Life," starting with stocks from large US companies and intermediate-term corporate bonds, which made the portfolio last longer than it would with the government bonds. We applied our Perfect Financial Storm Test, taking an initial annual 5.5% distribution at the start of the year, and increased that distribution by the inflation rate each year. That portfolio lasted only 17 years. That means that if you hope to live to 100, you'd have to work until you're 83 years old if you don't want to run out of money.

We went on to apply five more levels of diversification—still using the 60/40 blend, but diversifying the equities among international stocks and large- and small-cap US stocks with a healthy emphasis on value stocks. With those improvements our portfolio lasted 33 years if we don't include the outlier years, 1937 and 1969, or 23 years if we do. (See the table on page 119 in Chapter Nine, "Ten Steps to a Worry-Free Income for Life.")

It's only when we adjust the balance of our major asset classes to 70% stocks and 30% bonds that the portfolio lasts 40 years in 94% of the time frames we tested—that's up from 84% without that adjustment. When we include the time frames starting in 1937 and 1969 it was depleted in 24 years, but when we applied the 8-Year Rule even those passed the Perfect Financial Storm Test: our All-Weather Retirement Portfolio lasted 40 years 100% of the time.

Bottom line, I recommend the 70/30 blend because it gives you the best possible chance of having a worry-free income for the rest of your life—even if you retire at age 60 and live to be 100.

As an added benefit, by putting a smaller percentage of your money into bonds, you further reduce your exposure to inflation risk. Remember, when you own bonds, which pay you a fixed rate of interest, you stand to lose money if inflation is high (that is, your dollars are worth less) while you own those bonds. (See "Guaranteed Cash Investments" on page 40 in Chapter Four, "Investments 101.") So if 40% of your portfolio is in bonds, your exposure to that risk is higher than if you reduce that number to 30%.

With that said, a 60/40 blend certainly is less volatile, and it may help you sleep at night. If you're married and you and your spouse are both 70 or older, or you're single and 65 and feel comfortable with an income stream that's expected to last 30 years rather than 40, then the 60/40 blend might be the way to go. But if you want a portfolio that you can expect to last 40 years through a perfect financial storm, then I recommend you go with 70% stocks and 30% bonds.

Question #3. *"I would like to work with a fee-only advisor, but I've heard they have high minimum initial investments. What is the minimum amount they generally require? Should I ask for an initial consultation?"*

Fee-only advisors generally do require a minimum investment amount to start a relationship. That's the downside to using them. Since they don't make high commissions on the front end, they generally compensate by making sure they get paid enough dollars to cover their costs. The minimums vary widely, but $100,000 to $250,000 is common. In many cases if you are about to retire, say within 5 years, an advisor will help you during that time frame with minimal cost, with the understanding that when you retire you will use him as your advisor—if, of course, you have been pleased with his services up to that point.

Almost all quality advisors offer a free initial consultation. In that consultation, if he can help you he will show you how, and what your costs would be. If he can't help you at that time—whether because you can't meet his minimum investment requirement, you don't share the same investment philosophies, or simply because the two of you just don't click—chances are he'll share money-saving, tax-saving, and retirement preparation suggestions. Even if you're not ready to be a client at that point, you'll probably be able to tell if he is client oriented, and if you'd like to use him at some future date.

Before you go in for your initial consultation, reread Chapter Twelve, "Finding an Advisor You Can Trust." Or if you want more detail and a step-by-step approach to help you find a trustworthy advisor, check out the book that gives you exactly that: *The Worry-Free Retirement Guide to Finding a Trustworthy Financial Advisor*, by yours truly.

Question #4. *"I'm about to retire, and I can't afford to lose a penny. Why can't I just invest in CDs? They may not be making much, but at least I know I can't lose money."*

It's true that the value of a CD, before inflation, doesn't go down. It is also guaranteed by the government up to certain limits. But the *purchasing power* of a CD can in fact go down, and that is a real and potentially devastating financial risk.

The amount of money you have invested in that CD is less important than the amount of goods and services you can purchase with that money. Think about the price of a postage stamp 40 years ago—if you can. The price in 1980 was 15 cents. What is it now? In 1980 a dollar would buy you six postage stamps, with change left over. Today that same dollar won't even buy two stamps. That's the power of inflation and the impact it has on your purchasing power.

Now consider those CDs of yours as part of a 40-year retirement plan. The dollars you invest today will actually be worth far less in purchasing power 40 years from now—or even 5 or 10 years from now. What impact will that have on your income stream? If your money is in CDs, you will in effect "lose money" because of inflation. Whatever else your portfolio does for you, it must protect you against a period of high inflation because you lose so much purchasing power in those times. Of the various financial storms that are likely to come along during your retirement, this one can potentially do you the most harm. You need to prepare for this!

In my financial storm analysis of how various investments performed between 1973 and 2012 (see Chapter Seven, "The Perfect Financial Storm: Can You Survive It?")—one of the best times in history for CD rates—with a 5.5% distribution your money would only last for 24 years. Please keep in mind, this was *the best of times* for CDs. When we tested our All-Weather Retirement Portfolio through that same time period—*the worst of times* for equities—it lasted 40 years. In other words, the best of times for CDs still didn't beat the worst of times for the balanced, diversified equity and bond portfolio.

Question #5. *"I'm retiring later [or earlier] than age 60. Can I take more [or should I take less] than the 5.5% distribution?"*

Probably. The All-Weather Retirement Portfolio is designed to provide lifelong income for a 60-year-old retiree who expects to live to be 100—that is, it will last 40 years with an initial 5.5% distribution (adjusted for inflation each year). However, if you're already 65 when you set up your portfolio, you're probably willing to assume you won't need an income for 40 years, so you might as well enjoy having a bit more spending money in your pocket. And if you're lucky enough to retire at age 55, that money will need to last *longer than* 40 years. Either way, it makes sense to consider adjusting your initial distribution amount (which you'll adjust annually for inflation) accordingly.

First and foremost, we'll assume your money is invested using the asset allocation and the 8-Year Rule we identified in the All-Weather Retirement Portfolio. Here's my recommendation for the amount of money you can take out, depending on your age when you begin taking it, and still expect your portfolio to provide you with an income until your 100th birthday.

YOUR AGE WHEN YOU START TAKING A DISTRIBUTION	YOUR INITIAL DISTRIBUTION RATE
55	5.0%
60	5.5%
65	5.7%
70	5.9%

One note of caution: Keep in mind that these recommended rates are based on the assumption you'll live to be 100 years old. There's a real possibility you'll live longer than that, so don't fudge on these numbers. It's always better to err on the side of caution, so I would encourage you to start with a lower distribution rate if you can afford it.

Question #6. *"I'm single, 70, and plan to live to 100, so I only need my portfolio to last about 30 years. I don't need the extra distribution amount, but I would like to have a less volatile portfolio. What would you suggest?"*

If you want your portfolio to last 30 years with less volatility, you can adjust the 70/30 blend (70% equities and 30% bonds) to a 60/40 blend (60% equities and 40% bonds). But be sure to maintain the recommended distribution within each major asset class, with the equities balanced in favor of value stocks. Your basic 60/40 portfolio should look like this:

- 40% intermediate-term corporate bonds

- 42% US stocks

- 20% large-cap value

- 10% large-cap growth

- 12% small-cap value

- 18% international stocks

- 13% developed countries

- 5% emerging markets

As always, you'll need to rebalance the portfolio on a regular basis as we discussed in Chapter Ten, "Rebalancing Your Portfolio," starting on page 131.

Above all, keep in mind that the 60/40 blend does expose you more to inflation and interest rate risk. Please be sure to evaluate that scenario before you decide to go that route.

Question #7. *"But I want guarantees! I can't afford to lose money! I'm not able to go back to work, like I used to do. Isn't there something I can do with my money that's guaranteed?"*

You want something that can maintain your lifestyle, so there's no chance whatsoever that you will end up a bag lady.

When you consider the possibility of a bad inflationary time frame, the dollar collapsing completely, the stock market crashing and not coming back for an extended time frame, and so on … it's tough. Treasury bills are considered "risk free." A 6-month T-bill is currently paying 0.02%.[42] That means on a $100,000 investment you'd receive a whopping $20 a year. For every million dollars you invest, you'd receive $200. Unless you want to live off your principal and risk running out of money, that "guarantee" wouldn't provide you with much of a retirement income.

What I can offer you is this. I suggest your goal should be *how to maximize the probabilities* that no matter what happens in the outside world—and it's a given that that's tough to predict or control—you are going to be comfortable for the rest of your life.

To do so means you are giving up the chance for the big, home-run return. It also means you're not in a "guaranteed" investment that exposes you to inflation risk. What you're looking for is the sweet spot between the two, between the guaranteed investments and those that carry a higher risk.

---

42   As of June 3, 2021.

That means diversifying in a portfolio that has some volatility. It also means not letting your emotions get the best of you, and not taking bigger risks when your friends and neighbors tell you about the killing they are making in … whatever. It also means you don't dump your portfolio and put all your money in cash just because you have a negative year or two.

It is my sincere belief, at this time, that the best way to do this is through the plan I've shared with you in this book, diversifying in the asset classes I've suggested, in the mix I've suggested, and rebalancing as I've suggested.

Question #8. *"Are there ways to reduce taxation from the income stream?"*

Quite possibly. But there are so many potential ways to do it that I could write an entire volume on that subject alone. (I'm working on it!) It's beyond the scope of this book.

I will, however, suggest one of the most common tax-saving strategies.

1. First, calculate how much you expect to draw—that is, the dollar amount of your 5.5% disbursement—from all of your investment sources: IRAs, Roth IRAs, taxable investments … whatever you've got.

2. Then figure out which of your investment sources will be taxed the least—cash, after-tax investments, and so forth. (This can be a little bit of an art as well as a science. If you think the capital gains tax is going to go up in the next few years, you might want to take the income stream from that bucket—even though it's a taxable one—and pay at the current, lower capital gains rates. Of course, predicting fluctuations in capital gains

taxes is not an easy call, so it would be wise to discuss this with your financial advisor or tax specialist.)

3. Now, take the dollar amount you came up with in Step #1, and take *all* of that amount from the least-taxed source you identified in Step #2.

You also want to be sure to avoid tax traps. Currently, when you reach the age of 72 there is a 50% penalty (yes, you read that right) if you don't take the required minimum distribution out of your traditional IRAs and retirement plan balances. There are some exceptions, but in general the first year after you turn 72 your required distribution will be around 4% of the balance in your account; then it goes up each year based on life expectancy tables. (Your financial advisor will tell you what your minimum distribution is, or you can find out at the IRS website—just go to www.IRS.gov, and do a search for "required minimum distribution.")

The problem is, your traditional IRAs and retirement plans are generally the last places you want to take income—but of course you also don't want to be paying a 50% penalty. When you hit 72 you need to calculate the dollar amount of the minimum distribution, then bite the bullet and take that amount from your IRAs. Then you can take the rest of your year's distribution from other areas.

Unfortunately, determining how much to take from which accounts can become pretty complicated. If you have many different accounts, and multiple sources of taxable income, the required distribution rules can cause the number of different tax scenarios to increase exponentially. However, it's well worth exploring your options carefully, because the proper analysis can save you a bundle in taxes and penalties. Of course, if it all seems a bit mind numbing, this might be a good time to enlist the help of a good advisor.

Chapter Fifteen

You're Ready to Cast Off

A s I write the final pages of this book, it's my sincere hope that, for you, this is not the end but a beginning. I hope I've inspired you to continue your exploration of how you can make the most of your investments so your retirement years are free from worry and full of the enjoyment you so richly deserve. In these few pages I've distilled the best of what I've learned in more than 35 years of research and experience. It's been a labor of love, because it matters to me that you have the information you need to make the best possible choices about your retirement.

But that doesn't mean you should stop reading and learning. *Never stop learning!* There's a wealth of information available to you about all the things we've considered in this book. In fact, I'm confident that the more you study, the more you'll appreciate and feel comfortable with the strategies I've outlined for you here.

But where do you go from here? With so many resources out there, where can you find the information that will build on the knowledge you have now? There's no shortage of books with enticing titles, like *How to Get Rich the Quick and Easy Way with No Risk ... in Your Spare Time.* I must admit, I've read my share of those. (Confession is good for the soul, right?) Most are confusing or misleading or worse. But they sell well because, after all, everyone wants a quick fix.

But you and I know better. You already understand the principles of investing well enough to know there is no quick and easy, risk-free way to a worry-free income for life. Now you're ready to expand on that knowledge, and there are plenty of excellent books that will help you do exactly that.

Here's a list of my top nine recommendations. Enjoy.

***The Richest Man in Babylon* by George S. Clason.** Written in the 1930s, this book is still a bestseller. Not really an investment book, it is more of a fundamental money management book. It is the all-time classic in this area. At my firm we buy hundreds of copies of Clason's book to give away to our clients.

No matter what your age or financial situation, this is the book to read. Do you know someone struggling with debt? This is the book to give him. How about a young graduate? This is the book to give him. Only the very old and destitute would not benefit from Clason's insights.

***Simple Wealth, Inevitable Wealth* by Nick Murray.** This is another book we hand out to many of our clients to read. It shares many important principles, but one of the things it does best is put the inflation landmine into perspective. This is a big problem for many people, and lots of investors find it difficult to understand. Nick Murray does a great job of explaining exactly why you need equities in your portfolio, and why CDs are probably going to be a disaster.

***Winning the Loser's Game: Timeless Strategies for Successful Investing* by Charles D. Ellis.** A great book! It studies market timing, stock selection, and how to reduce your liability exposure. The book is thin, and it used to be expensive. When it came out it cost about $95. Fortunately it's in paperback now for far less, but even if it did cost $95, it would be worth every penny.

Why Smart People Make Big Money Mistakes and How to Correct Them: Lessons from the Life-Changing Science of Behavioral Economics **by Gary Belsky and Thomas Gilovich.** This book talks about the biggest factor in play when investors and advisors don't get reasonable investment returns: their behavior is driven by emotion. Emotions have a big impact on investor success. In fact, the authors explain why emotion-driven behavior is a bigger factor than all the others ... combined. It's a great book and an easy read.

Asset Allocation: Balancing Financial Risk **by Roger Gibson.** Terrific book. Gibson explains how to design a portfolio to maximize the expected return and minimize the expected risk through proper diversification. It is probably the classic in the industry, if you believe in asset allocation (and you should if you want to stay afloat).

Should you include real estate investment trusts (REITs) in your portfolio? What are the benefits of proper diversification? How do you achieve it? Should you try to time the market? What types of risk do you need to be concerned with? The answers to all these questions and much more can be found in Gibson's book.

The Prudent Investor's Guide to Beating Wall Street at Its Own Game **by John J. Bowen Jr., and Daniel C. Goldie.** If you had millions of dollars' worth of investment data and decades to test ideas, you would probably come up with the conclusions outlined in this book. Bowen has taken academic research and distilled it down to fundamental concepts. There's not any hype. As *Dragnet*'s Sergeant Friday used to say (you do remember *Dragnet*, don't you?), "Just the facts, ma'am." You will see a lot of parallels between his book and the one you're holding.

Classics: An Investor's Anthology **edited by Charles D. Ellis.** If you had all the time in the world to read the various financial publications issued since 1920, and could clip out the best articles, those that have withstood the test of time … you would have this book. Charles Ellis has done it for you. A tremendous effort.

Be sure to read Harry Markowitz's work in the chapter called "Portfolio Selection." The article was written in the 1950s, and he won a Nobel Prize in the 1990s with this investment philosophy.

The Psychology of Investing **by John R. Nofsinger.** This is fun and easy to read and, like *Why Smart People Make Big Money Mistakes,* it shows the natural tendency of people to make mistakes with their investments because of behavior and the psychology of money. A fun, great book.

Happy Money: The Science of Happier Spending **by Elizabeth Dunn and Michael Norton.** It's about how to spend your money to maximize your happiness factor. The authors demonstrate how money can in fact buy happiness if you follow their five core principles of smart spending.

There are also certain authors that I think are solid, and anything they write on the topic of investing for retirement is worthy. Here's a short list:

1. Charles Ellis

2. Nick Murray

3. Roger Gibson

4. Dave Ramsey

5. Benjamin Graham

6. Randy Thurman (of course!)

In closing, the single most important message I'd like to share with you is this: Keep reading, keep studying ... keep learning. I know I will. In fact, as the years pass, there will probably be refinements in my recommendations on how you manage your portfolio. Watch for updates. And if you found this book beneficial, please share it with others so you can help them, too, enjoy a worry-free income for life.

> **The single most important message I'd like to share with you is this: Keep reading, keep studying ... keep learning.**

About the Author

Randy L. Thurman started in the financial planning business in 1986, and has since become widely recognized as one of the top financial advisors in the United States. He specializes in helping those who have retired (or are about to retire) have a comfortable income for life. He is a Certified Public Accountant (CPA) and a Certified Financial Planner™ professional, also known as a CFP® professional. He is also a Personal Financial Specialist (PFS), a credential that recognizes CPAs with additional experience and expertise in financial planning. PFS candidates must pass a technical exam and complete rigorous continuing education requirements. Randy holds four degrees, including an MBA from Oklahoma State University, and has taught investing, personal finance, and economics at the college level.

In 1990 Randy founded his firm, Financial Planning Company of Oklahoma, which in 1997 merged with Retirement Investment Advisors, Inc. He continues today as chief executive officer. Under his leadership the firm has become one of the largest fee-only investment advisory firms in Oklahoma, with over a billion dollars in assets under management. All the advisors of the firm are CFP® professionals and/or CPA/PFS.

As a result of 35 years of dedication and commitment to excellence in financial planning, Randy is frequently lauded as one of the nation's most trusted investment advisors. As of this writing, he and his firm have been cited 43 times as among the best in the country in national and local publications such as *Worth* magazine, *Medical Economics*, *Bloomberg Wealth Manager Magazine*, *Financial Times*, *Financial Advisor Magazine*, AdvisoryHQ, Expertise.com, and J. K. Lasser's books on estate planning.[43]

Randy has also been recognized at the local level for excellence and leadership, including:

- Oklahoma Business Ethics Compass Award,

- Oklahoma Society of CPAs award for Outstanding CPA in Financial Planning,

- The Journal Record Beacon Award, Charitable Influence: Small Business, and

- The Journal Record 2021 Power List: The 30 Most Influential People in Banking and Finance.

Over the years, Randy has shared his expertise and insight as the author of five books and an extensive list of articles on financial planning, investing, and business ethics. His book *The All-Weather Retirement Portfolio: Your Post-Retirement Guide to a Worry-Free Income for Life* provides time-tested guidance for financial peace of mind, while *One More Step: The 638 Best Quotes for the Runner* inspires runners and others to realize their goals. His articles have appeared in *CPAFocus*, *Medical Economics*, *NW Style Magazine*, *405 Magazine*, *Metro Journal*, *The Oklahoman*, and others. He is much sought after as a speaker for conferences, workshops, and broadcast media, including

---

43   A complete and up-to-date list, including criteria, is available upon request.

appearances on Fox News Channel's *Fox on Money* and as the former host of the weekly radio program *Money Talks*.

Randy is also active as a volunteer in his community, and in 2005 received the Oklahoma Society of CPAs' Public Service Award. He is a member of the South Oklahoma City Rotary Club and sits on the boards, or is a trustee, of six nonprofit organizations, including the Oklahoma State University Board of Governors, the Investment Committee of the YMCA of Greater Oklahoma City, the Oklahoma City Community College Foundation, and the Oklahoma City Employee Retirement System.

Most importantly, Randy is a family man who treasures time with his wife and son. He's an active member of his church community and an enthusiastic reader, writer, and runner.

For more information about Randy L. Thurman's work, and to contact him, visit his website at www.RandyThurman.com.

Acknowledgments

Many people and, in this case, companies, make a book possible. I'd love to share all their names, but that, in and of itself, would be a book—especially if I wrote all about them and how they helped. Since space doesn't allow me to list everyone, please know that if you helped me … I'm grateful.

Pati, my wife of 31 years. The most positive, upbeat, and energetic person I know. Anyone who can wake up at 4:30 a.m., energetic and happy to go run in the hills, is maybe a bit crazy, but a good crazy.

Jan Allegretti. My wonderful editor for 14 years now. We drive each other crazy on occasion but, like every good team, we work together to deliver a great product for the reader. Not only does she edit, but she offers great advice on cover design, readability, formatting, etc. Without her, this book would not have been readable or, for that matter, possible.

Heather Misialek. My personal assistant for 15 years and all-time amazing person. She must be an angel to put up with me (I'm not always the easiest person to work for). She knows what I am about to think before I think it. My work and personal life are better because of her. Thank you, Heather!

Carol Ringrose Alexander. An outstanding advisor at our firm for 18 years. She has helped me with my writing using her extensive writing experience. She read through the manuscript and offered numerous outstanding suggestions.

Brenda Bolander. Another outstanding advisor at our firm in her tenth year. Our firm's compliance officer. She's read through the manuscript numerous times for regulatory issues.

Andrew Flinton. My business partner and one of the smartest people I know. Not only is he a great advisor, but he is an even better person.

Jimmy J. Williams. Co-speaker with me at many Oklahoma Society of CPAs and AICPA Advanced Personal Financial Planning conferences. I helped Jimmy get started in the investment advisory business, and then he helped me get better.

John Burbrick, a fan of the first edition of this book. He looked over Chapter Nine and made some great suggestions.

Megan Elger, who designed the cover. After 7 months of me changing my mind, asking for different options, sharing reader polling, raising image issues, and more, she weathered it all with professionalism. The end result was outstanding. Great job.

Nate Best, ForbesBooks editor who offered many outstanding suggestions.

Roger Ibbotson. Some call him the father of asset allocation. I heard him speak when he was a professor at Yale University, and he inspired me to read and study more.

Roger Gibson. Great speaker and author of the book *Asset Allocation: Balancing Financial Risk*, the first book I read on the topic. He helped me become passionate about asset allocation and what it can do for retirees.

Charles Ellis. Author of one of the best investment books ever written, *Investment Policy: How to Win the Loser's Game*. This is the book that started my insatiable quest to read and learn in this area.

Bob Veres. His newsletter, *Inside Information*, led me to Roger Gibson and the book *Asset Allocation*. His provocative look at the industry always causes me to ponder and think.

Nick Murray. Speaker and author. Wrote the great investment book *Simple Wealth, Inevitable Wealth*. Stressed the importance of equities, protecting against inflation, and avoiding the big mistake.

Morningstar. The provider of the data in the *Ibbotson SBBI Classic Yearbook*. What a great source of information!

Global Financial Data. Data provider that allowed me to go back before 1970 on several asset classes. I wouldn't have a second edition without them.

SEI Private Trust Co. The primary custodian where we place our clients' funds, and we use their Y-share mutual funds to a large degree. Outstanding group that has shared much research and many thoughts over the years.

Dimensional Fund Advisors (DFA). Another great group of funds with a tremendous amount of research. Love their research and insights.

Mom. She took me to the library to get my library card around age two. I started reading then and haven't stopped since.

And of course, my clients over the past 35 years, who encouraged me and trusted me with their life savings.

Index